Other Side of Succession

How to Boost the Value of Your Business
up to 70 Percent in Five Years or Less,
Get Out of the Day to Day
or Sell Out, Take the Money & Run

Nick,

Jim Grew

Best,

Jim

The Other Side of Succession
Design by Jerry Fletcher
Printed in USA

Accelerate Publications
2327 NW Northrup, Portland OR 97210

Library of Congress Cataloging-in-Publication Data

Grew, James W.
The Other Side of Succession: How To Boost the
Value of Your Business up to 70 Percent in Five Years or
Less Get Out of the Day to Day or Sell Out, Take the Money
& Run/by Jim Grew
168 Pages
Includes bibliographical references and index.
ISBN 978-0-692-61403-7
1.Executive Succession 2. Leadership 3. Management
4. Organizational Effectiveness I. Title

HD 38.2 G 2016 Version 1

DISCLAIMER

This book details the author's personal experiences with and opinions about business operations. The author is neither an attorney, nor a licensed financial consultant.

The author and publisher are providing this book and its contents on an "as is" basis and make no representations or warranties of any kind with respect to this book or its contents. The author and publisher disclaim all such representations and warranties, including for example warranties of merchantability and financial advice for a particular purpose. In addition, the author and publisher do not represent or warrant that the information accessible via this book is accurate, complete or current.

The statements made about products and services have not been evaluated by the U.S. government. Please consult with your own attorney, Certified Public Accountant or financial/business services professional regarding the suggestions and recommendations made in this book.

Except as specifically stated in this book, neither the author or publisher, nor any authors, contributors, or other representatives will be liable for damages arising out of or in connection with the use of this book. This is a comprehensive limitation of liability that applies to all damages of any kind, including (without limitation) compensatory; direct, indirect or consequential damages; loss of data, income or profit; loss of or damage to property and claims of third parties.

You understand that this book is not intended as a substitute for consultation with a licensed financial professional. Before you begin any financial program, or change your lifestyle in any way, you will consult a licensed financial professional to ensure that you are doing what's best for your financial condition.

This book provides content related to business topics, finances and economic living. As such, use of this book implies your acceptance of this disclaimer.

For my parents, Don and Bernice Grew, who drove to Portland in 1927 in a Model T Ford built by my dad from junk-yard parts. With a high school education and a vigorous will to succeed, their thirst for learning and willingness to help all comers pulled them and hundreds of others into successive rich life experiences beyond even their ambitious dreams.

Acknowledgments

The entrepreneurial spirit that fueled my mom and dad is alive and well 88 years later, driving the hundreds of leaders who have built successful businesses all over the country. Their will and grit have produced a remarkable trail of business and life opportunities for thousands of families. They, like all of us, had help along the way.

I salute some of the many folks who have given me a hand and helped me along this path.

Thanks to my first consulting clients — Barb and Tom Miller — as well as clients, friends, and mentors, especially Larry Pexton, Rick Pay, Phil Symchych, Alan Weiss, Manoj Garg, Nicole Thibodeau, Heidi Pozzo, Bill Mascott, David Jones, John Hoglund, Jerry Vieira, Bruce Hazen, Ethan Dunham, Norm Duffett and Bob and Shirley Grew.

I especially want to thank my wife (and night psychiatrist) Dr. Leslie Neilson, for hundreds of pithy insights that make me look wiser than I am and for the kind of marriage and support that books are written about. Also special thanks to my editor, Nina Taylor, and copy thinker–marketing whiz Jerry Fletcher, whose firm guidance carried me well beyond what I imagined was possible.

You have all been remarkable teachers and friends.

Table of Contents

Table of Contents (continued)

Foreword

Don't even think about getting out of your business before you read this book.

Early on in my career an attorney friend explained the reality of starting a company. She said, *"Any fool can start a business and with a little luck be successful... But getting out is the hard part."*

Getting out *is* the hard part.

Believing in "Purchase Fairies" is not an answer (see The Fourth Way).

Getting bottled up in minutiae will cause you to miss the big picture.

Not knowing what you're going to do when every day is a Saturday is a major project without a plan.

This is not the sort of problem you grapple with every day.

This book and Jim's wisdom can help you find answers.

**What is on the other side of the exit is *your choice.*
**An exit strategy is only half the equation. That dark room that awaits you on the other side of the door could be the opportunity of a lifetime for you and others.

You need to take into account all the individuals your decisions will impact.

The Other Side of Succession

And you need to do so before you go through the door.

This book and Jim's wisdom can help you exit in style.

Whether you keep a hand in or take the money and run is *for you to choose.*

No matter what age you consider your options, you should look at all of them.

A complete sell out can be to a partner, your family, your employees, an outside buyer, a consortium, or competitor.

A partial sale can alleviate day-to-day responsibilities while assuring all concerned that the business will go on.

Investigate the choices. Let yourself excel in succession as you have in business.

This book and Jim's wisdom can help you make the right choices.

Will YOU write the story of your legacy?

All of us that build businesses leave a legacy. You have a choice: Write it yourself or let it be written by others.

Want the family to continue in the business? Make it so.

Want the principled approach you brought to this enterprise to stand longer? Find a way to do it.

Want the employees to be certain of their jobs? Make it part of an agreement.

Jim Grew

This book and Jim's wisdom can help you write your legacy.

Jim's wisdom, distilled in this book can help you with the big decisions.

It will not get into the infinite details of mergers and acquisitions.

It will not discuss how to negotiate a deal or write the agreement or look good for the due diligence.

It will tell you how to strategize your succession and how to make your business more successful and desirable regardless of what you decide.

This book and Jim's wisdom can help you with your strategic approach to the other side of the door.

Jerry Fletcher, CEO

The Fourth Way

If you're over 50 and own your business, you're special. You're special because you have a lifesaving choice in front of you, if you'll see it and seek it. It's okay, you'll be safe reading this—it's not a motivational piece. Instead, it's a peek around the corner at a life you may not have imagined. Here's the story:

The Peak Myth

We're flooded with stories of entrepreneurs who make it big before they're 40. The YPO (Young Presidents Organization) memorializes them. Stories of legendary founders (Gates, Hsieh, Jobs) suggest that the life curve of a business builder is slow start, steep up, and a continuing upward trajectory like a missile with explosive launch power. Little is written about their lives after 50. We imagine it as a mix of wealth, toys, celebration and...

The truth is different. Since each leader charts her own path, her life curve is special. Most successful folks suffer heartbreaking failures in their path to success, and they don't know how their story will turn out until it turns out. Regardless of their platform, when they turn 50 a life fact seeps into their soul: it all will end. Not yet. But it will.

The Peak Reality

We're waist deep in folks who reignited at 50 to produce their greatest life work:
• Lou Gerstner turned around IBM starting at 51 years old.
• Warren Buffett earned 99 percent of his wealth after age 50.

- Henry Kissinger received the Nobel Peace Prize at age 50.
- Meg Whitman became CEO at Hewlett Packard at age 56. (Okay, the results aren't in yet.)

SPEED BUMP: If you've hit 50, the peak is before you, not behind you.

The Peak Choice:
Which of these business leaders will you be after you're 50?

- **Clutcher:** This owner hangs on for dear life, celebrating the best strategies that he's learned in his business lifetime. He and his business seep slowly away, with a lingering sense of regret. A local business, legendary for its success in making precision parts for an international vehicle manufacturer, survived two crisis points by cutting past the bone. When it lost a big chunk of business at the 2009 recession, it looked back instead of forward, cutting past the bone again. Its progressive employee layoffs destroyed its heart and mind, and it closed.
- **Coaster:** This owner has his life finally working, with all its perks: community respect, business success, time and money for toys and play, good friends, and more. He'll sell eventually, he thinks, but now is no time to be thinking dark thoughts. Customers and employees detect a subtle slide in the urgency and pride that built their success.
- **Chaser:** He's always chased the next big thing, and now it's the home run sale of his business. He's heard of folks who sell quickly to an industry insider for huge sums, with little pain. He gazes longingly at the happy life without the pain of being an owner-manager. This is fairyland, and he even knows it, sort of. Tough challenges never stopped him before, so he keeps on with it. His chances are slim and none.

SPEED BUMP: The fourth way is sitting there waiting for you to pick it up.

What's the fourth way? Be who you are: an **Igniter**. You have the gift to turn on customers and employees. You've built a successful business out of your head. It succeeded because of you, not because of chance. Of course you had help and luck and support. All successful people do. The difference in your company is you, so look that in the face and ask the Serena Williams question.

SPEED BUMP: What will win now?

Thirty-two-year-old female professional tennis players are coaches, not Grand Slam winners. Serena decided to channel her smarts and drive to win with her wits, not her speed. Back to the Igniter: Since you're at peak skill, knowledge, power, and influence in your business, why not harvest that? Why not find a way to double the value of your business in five years, cut your stress, work less, and have the jolt of fun at building again? It's life at its richest, and you'll enrich everyone around you at the same time!

Succession — and this book— is not what you think. It's not about any of these:
- Selling your business
- Preparing your business for sale
- Exiting your life

It is about what can be the richest and most gratifying period in your life, if you'll follow the rules that you already know:
- A big payoff requires preparation.
- Shortcuts are vital, since there's never enough time.
- Expert help makes the difference between adequate and rewarding.

The Other Side of Succession

So here are the first rules for success:
- See succession as a process that will last at least several years; it's not an event.
- Re-recruit the vital 25-year-old that you really are.
- Make space to dream.

Things to avoid (since we're in the rules business for a while):
- Stop thinking about selling your business (look at it from the corner of your eye, like a star at night).
- Stop planning your retirement. The only planning that it needs is wealth.
- Stop thinking about how to "get out." We all get out when we're dead. That comes to us in spite of our plans, and it doesn't need our help.

Bonus Fantasy

The purchase fairy has done more damage to owners' lives and retirements than anything — other than greed and stupidity. purchase fairy? That's the fantasy that unlike all others, you are so special that a man will ride up on a white horse and make you a full-price, all-cash, no-contingency offer for your business, and then push the money across the table to you.

Blow up the idea of a purchase fairy. The barn is empty of white-horse saviors, and purchase fairies have always existed only in the minds of business owners who are amateur sellers. Why would you join them?

And for now, blow up the idea of selling your business, regardless of the emergency that's just raised its head. You wouldn't have sold for this bad of a deal when you were 25, so why would you do so now?

So what DOES the smart guy do (smart woman and smart

XVI

person included)?
- Look closely at the wonderful business that you've built, and the reasons why customers and employees want to share their lives and their wealth with you.
- Use that look to imagine the next big thing (NBT) for your business.
- Pull in the team to help you make that NBT happen in your lifetime. Why not?

Here's what we'll do in this book:
- Help you frame your NBT (Next Big Thing).
- Help you bring your NBT into the context of your life today.
- Present a menu of tips and tricks that will boost you along your way.

ACCELERANT: Read this little book. It will open the door to a future you'll love.

Cash Flow Genie

Why do you think that even though you've worked 60-hour weeks (or more) for 20 years or more to build your business, you can step back and the cash flow will continue? How can that make any sense? Either you weren't needed (unlikely most of the time) or you will have to have an equally competent replacement.

SPEED BUMP: How will you protect future cash flow?

Yes, this is for founders of successful firms who are over 50 and thinking about their next steps. It seems like an obviousity, but somehow this question is frequently clouded in the daily swirl. Worse, actions (legal, financial, and family) that retirement demands add layers of difficulty to daily operations and planning. The magical assumption is that cash flow has always been there, and "my team" will keep it coming.

SPEED BUMP: Replacing you is harder than you think. Who cares about this cash flow? Here's a starter list:
1. You
2. Your family
3. Your employees
4. Your customers
5. Your suppliers
6. Potential investors
7. Potential buyers

John Doerr is a legendary venture capitalist. As founder and leader of Kleiner Perkins (KP), likely one of the top three VC firms in Silicon Valley, he finds himself at a strange place at age 64. He's the lead investor in firms like Google, Amazon, Genentech, Sun Microsystems, and Netscape.* That means he made the key investment at a very early stage. Here's his dilemma: How does his firm (KP) thrive as he steps back?

Right now, he faces these pressures:
- Top talent is moving to other firms, worried that there is no room for them.
- Investors are hesitating to place their money with KP, when his status is uncertain.
- Leadership of his firm is fuzzy, and it needs to be sharpened up fast.
- Recruitment to maintain the top talent that drives success is much tougher than it was.

SPEED BUMP: You are more like KP than you ever imagined.

KP actually faces shrinking investment funds, and is sorting out new leadership to prevent their demise!

Here is your challenge: As your presence shrinks (voluntarily or not), people in and out of the business will act on their assumptions about their future. Unless you begin to create the story about the future of the business, they'll assume it's at least dangerous for them, if not deadly. The "story" is your plan, of course. These people will read the plan in their own interest first, and then in the company's interest. They will put themselves into your story as they understand it.

SPEED BUMP: Unless you share your plan, folks will write their own story.

To be successful, your plan must include these elements:

1. Leadership succession plan: Who will be the leaders of the key parts of the business and when will that happen? Usually, folks will know you're stepping back before the replacements are finalized. That's okay, if you acknowledge their interest and your commitment to making and implementing a plan to secure the future of the business.

2. Communication plan: This is a commitment that you'll communicate with your three essential groups as you form your plan. They don't expect it to emerge fully formed, but they do expect to be kept in the loop.

3. Reinvigoration of values: Now is the time to spool up the essential elements that have made your culture a success, like this:
- Create a new measure or two
- Task a leader or two with boosting one or two key elements

The Other Side of Succession

> • Charge your team with crafting a powerful sales initiative

These build on the experience that the best way to keep an adolescent out of trouble is to keep her busy. (It works with adults, if the goals are exciting).

ACCELERANT: How big a challenge will you give your team now?

Part 1 Sieze the Day

Chapter 1
Will Succession Be Your Greatest Midlife Crisis?

Black Box Warning: This aims at your emotions. That promises both power and pain, or at least discomfort. Continue at your peril—and your promise. (*A black box warning is the strictest warning label of a prescription drug by the FDA when there is reasonable evidence of a serious hazard with the drug.*)

If you are over 50 and own your business, here is some guidance you can't afford to ignore: Succession promises change—and growth—if you'll let it. The form of succession—retirement, selling your business, or handing your business to your son or daughter—doesn't matter for this discussion. What matters is how you approach it, and whether you seek the personal growth that's waiting there for you.

Here's the challenge: As we grow, we restrict our lives. Doors close, and we tend to be attracted to the familiar. By definition, that's a shrinking menu of choices. Our brains are wired to seek initial solutions vigorously and calmly maintain those solutions in the face of overwhelming opportunity to change. It's not about discipline; it's about your personal reality.

The Other Side of Succession

The pinch is in realizing this double hit:
• We're aging (eventually dying, and leaving everything).
• We deny aging.

SPEED BUMP: The combination of restriction and denial yields limited choices.

How can we blow up the limits safely enough to act? Consider this child-rearing nugget: Instead of taking a ring from a baby, offer an especially appealing glittering ball. She'll reach for the ball and drop the ring. It's time to recruit your child again.

SPEED BUMP: The business choice: Go big or get out.

The benefits of a dramatically more successful business are so striking that we wonder what keeps most owners from jumping for them. The answers:
• Fear of loss
• Avoiding sacrifice instead of seeking fulfillment
• Hanging on instead of letting go to grab the next rung

Ten years ago these were hurdles to be jumped with fear and excitement. Today they've become just hurdles for many, who rationalize with limits like these:
• I don't have time to make it back if I lose it all.
• I'm tired and I don't want to do it anymore.
• I'm fine. Leave me alone.

SPEED BUMP: Entropy will erode your position unless you act.

Before all that you've built is taken from you, choose how you choose to keep it. The most powerful choice is to grow it, inviting others into your inner circle to share the rewards

4

and do most of the work.

A long-time friend, now in his 60s, has moved from ignoring the future to igniting the most dramatic growth in his 30-year-old firm's history and experiencing all the excitement that comes with it. In parallel he's now able to explore ways to make his business endure, while serving his employees, his customers, and his family. He's as excited as I've ever seen him as he reaches for the glittering ball.

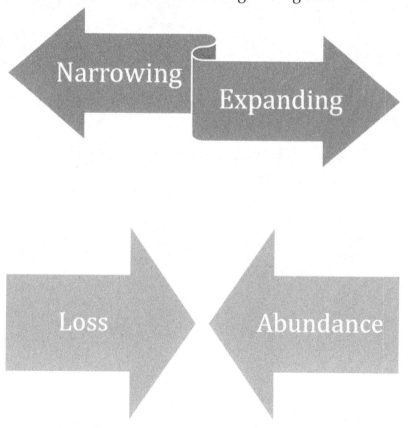

ACCELERANT: Will your future possibilities be a resource or a limitation?

Jim has prepared short videos for you that quickly highlight the information in each chapter.

View this video and all the others in the Succession Series on Jim's YouTube channel.

Chapter 2
Emergency Room Succession

Men are generally slower to acknowledge medical problems (and personal problems?) than women. Regardless, if there weren't an ER, many folks would never seek help — with terrible consequences. It's called URGENT care for a reason. The trigger to get us to Urgent Care is likely a problem that hurts so much we can't get through the day anymore. Often that trip should have happened earlier than it did.

SPEED BUMP: Avoiding issues with big consequences is easier than facing them.

Few of us believe "it" will happen to us, regardless of the "it." While this displacement helps us focus on what's in front of us, a useful life requirement, it also helps us avoid actions that can save pain, disappointment, and sometimes money. No, I'm not selling life insurance here.

SPEED BUMP: For a business leader, "it" is moving to being a part-timer.

Giving up what has driven and enthralled you for most of your adult life — your business — will put a lump in your throat. When it's described as becoming an investor, or becoming chairman of the board, it sounds more appealing,

7

but it's still easy to put off. In fact, because we're "pre-ER," it's easy to delay it, with the rationalization of the day.

SPEED BUMP: In succession, time is enemy number one.

My client Bill finds himself in a situation that's typical of many business owners. Do you see yourself in his Ten-Point Dilemma?
1. Over 50.
2. Financially successful.
3. Business more successful than he ever imagined.
4. He doesn't want to sell the business.
5. He doesn't want to die in the saddle.
6. Bonus: His top three executives, critical to the business, are older than he is.
7. Any of them may leave the business in the next 24 months.
8. There is no replacement for any of those three today, nor is there a plan to produce them.
9. No one else can train their replacements very well.
10. Asking them to train their replacement may trigger their exit.
For now, he's waiting until he sees a clear path forward. Waiting is not in his interest.

How to find the urgency before it's an emergency? Try these three steps:
1. Put your situation into words. Saying it aloud helps make it real, and it gets you thinking about possible answers. It's defining a problem like you do when you delegate success-fully, except that you're delegating to yourself.

2. Find an advisor outside the business whose wisdom you trust. Trusted wisdom on any topic can power up your options and help you sidestep fluffy danger. Self-delusion becomes a comfortable enemy.

SPEED BUMP: Avoid advisors who are deep but narrow. Broad is essential to expand your life menu (the agenda now).

3. Ask for options, not solutions. The variety of choices changes your approach to solutions, enabling a richer array in the discovery process. Due diligence here offers a huge ROI if the options are powerful enough.

ACCELERANT: What advisor will you call this week?

WORDS

ADVISOR

ACTION

OPTIONS

Succession & Your Peak

The Other Side of Succession

View the video on YouTube

Chapter 3
Real Time

The worst fantasy of folks over 50 is that they're going to die. It's the worst not because they're not going to die (we all will), but because they start "working on it" ahead of time! Working on it takes the form of wimping out, with thoughts like this: Since I'm going to die anyway, I'll coast. It'll feel wonderful to have no place to go and no one tugging on me. Stop the bad fantasies. Now. Instead, face these facts about you, as the owner-leader of a business:

Fact 1: Your Knowledge and Skill Are at an All-Time High
You have unmatched knowledge of customers, markets, suppliers, the weak spots in your business, and of which of your folks really can deliver more and want to (as well as those who can't). Notice how often you have to explain the obvious to your best employees. Why is that?

A Canadian friend and I were having a beer on his screened-in porch on a balmy September evening. It was delightfully quiet, until the roar of a lawn mower blasted us all. My friend turned and said, "I love to pay people to do work for me, so I don't have to do it."

He's figured out that he'd rather do other things, including sit and have a beer. You're surrounded with folks who'd

11

love to be doing some of the work you think you can't do without.

Notice how often you know how the financials will turn out before they're published. That exquisite sense can pay off big, if you'll shift your focus to a possible investment in growth. Investment always includes risk, which means foggy vision into the future. Your instinct is the best fog-cutter around, for your business. Use it to help your team craft a competitive advantage that delivers dramatic results.

SPEED BUMP: Success can come through your leadership, not just your skill.

Fact 2: Laser Learning Is What You Do Now
You ignore waste and focus on top issues. As a student in school, I was terrified of a bad grade, so I studied way past a reasonable payoff. As a result, my pool and volleyball skills were among the worst in my frat. Now I (and you) can look into opportunities, cull the gems, and drop the rest. Where depth is needed, we can either deep dive or get help.

It's not that you learn faster; it's that culling will dramatically shorten the list of things to learn. That yields overall speed, and the satisfaction that comes with it.

SPEED BUMP: Knowing what to skip is more important than knowing what to do.

Fact 3: Your Skill and Experience Pull the Odds of Success toward You
Real payoffs in business and sports come from beating the odds just a bit. Dramatic success comes from having and using your slight edge. You don't have to be an expert in ev-

erything, and everything doesn't have to work out all right. It's always a close call; the decision usually goes to skill. Luck comes and goes; but judgment wins.

In this game, you are more like the house than a player in a gambling casino. Your odds are likely the best they'll be in your life. Best of all, we'll show you how to use your advantage with a minimum of personal effort.

SPEED BUMP: Successful people aren't successful all the time; just enough of the time.

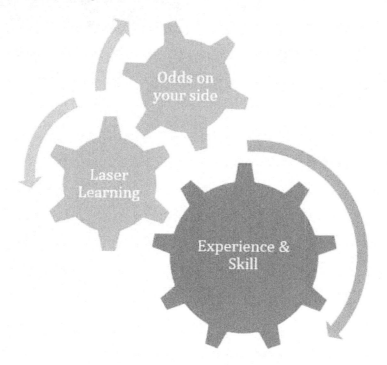

ACCELERANT: What are you going to do with all this?

You're a loaded gun!

Chapter 4
Build a Bigger Boat

When should you sell your company? If Mark Zuckerberg struggled with that question about Facebook, why do you think it's an easy question? He may be younger and richer, but the tradeoff is the same: When do I trade the thrill of ownership and its personal potential for the financial security and options that come with it?

The best answer: Not yet.

Instead, follow these three steps to move your focus away from selling, and toward an even better future:
1. Push out your earliest "sell date" at least five years.
2. Reignite your drive and skills.
3. Actively build your business, like you did years ago.

SPEED BUMP: Build the valuation of your business, not just sales or profit.

Imagine your business valuation as a boat that will do at least these things for you:
1. Support you and your family as you change your role in the business.
2. Help build your legacy in your business.
3. Continue to build your legacy in your community.

15

The Other Side of Succession

4. Provide for your family.
5. Enable your business to thrive with its new leadership.
6. Provide some survival cushion for your business when it hits future bumps.
7. Deliver the fun you've promised yourself all your life.

The striking truth: Your key advisors will stop the leaks in your boat, which is critical, but that is all they can do. Here's a starter overview of their services:

• An effective tax and estate attorney will see that you don't lose money in taxes that you don't need to pay, and help define the allocation of your assets when they are distributed to others to minimize future expensive friction.
• Your CPA will help you manage taxes and provide the information essential to effective business operation.
• A business attorney will help you structure the elements of your business to enhance their value if you should sell it.
• Your financial advisor will help make the best possible use of your investable assets, enabling them to retain value and grow as your involvement diminishes.

This planning is essential to avoid waste and the fighting that can turn your lifework into an excruciating melodrama for your family and employees. Remarkably, however, it misses one of the biggest opportunities of your life.

SPEED BUMP: You can block losses while you build your boat dramatically.

The secret is this: instead of slowing down, speed up the growth and success of your business, and get others to do most of the work!

Here's a pattern to help you grow this boat to multiples of your current business valuation:

$$BB = G + L$$

Translation: A bigger boat comes from growth and leadership.

To take it apart:

- Growth is revenue growth fueling improved profit.
- Leadership is the intentional development of a leadership team and general manager that can successfully operate your business and grow it.
- Your role shifts from owner-operator to investor who architects this transformational opportunity for yourself and your top leaders.

SPEED BUMP: Start on your boat five years before you plan to disembark.

Imagine your office door. Now think about stepping through that door to the next phase of your life. You're going to do it; it's a matter of when, not if. Why not set up that door to lead you to an even better life than you dreamed? Even better, there are several doors to choose from, allowing you more impact on your future than you thought possible.

The Other Side of Succession

Here are the doors:

Door #1:   Leave the business as it is today.
Door #2:   Grow 5 percent per year for four years.
Door #3:   Build a management team.
Door #4:   Build a general manager.

Remarkably, you can actually go through them in succession, and benefit from as many as you want to. Each door can enhance your business valuation by as much as your current EBITDA! If you can get to Door #4, you'll nearly double the valuation of your business. This extra return is on top of your annual income from the business, of course.

Here's what it might look like if your annual profit before tax is $1,000,000. Start with converting your profit to valuation, as in the figure, below.

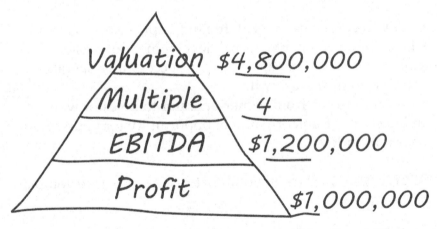

Valuation	$4,800,000
Multiple	4
EBITDA	$1,200,000
Profit	$1,000,000

Then explore how you might boost your valuation with the Doorway Steps that follow:

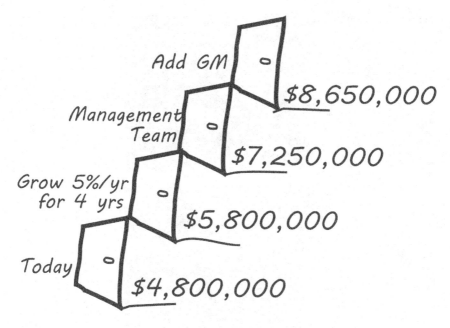

To calculate your numbers, adjust the earnings number to your own, and use the same multiplier.

Bonus: If you start soon enough, you can test-drive your choices, instead of making a forced choice (sell or keep the business). In fact, you don't need to decide whether or not to sell. Instead, if you choose from the doors above and do it five years before the soonest you'd sell anyway, you've just created a wonderful new life opportunity that was not even visible before!

ACCELERANT: Which door will you create and step through?

Part 2 Planning and Cultivating Growth

Chapter 5
Sprint Through the Tape

A curious thing happens as successful CEOs contemplate succession: They cede control to specialists and shut their eyes to possible bad surprises. This is similar to moving early to a retirement home, so I call it Retirement Home Thinking (RHT). A retirement home is a blessing at the right time: it offers safety and comfort—but at the cost of major limits and lost control. Engaging in RHT too early is like coasting to the finish line in a race: it guarantees a loss.

Most discussion about succession assumes that good legal and financial plans, and maybe a psychologist for the family, mean smooth sailing. But that formula guarantees loss—the only question is how much!

You would never dream of putting your house up for sale without careful preparation, often including upgrading, to get the best possible price. Yet this shortcutting is what leaders often do in planning their succession. They narrow their focus to legal and financial plans and let the business continue to run. How can the same person who built a successful business over decades suddenly put this complexity on autopilot?

SPEED BUMP: Legal and financial plans plug leaks and minimize pain, but nothing builds your quality of life like building your business.

A close business associate with 30 years' experience in the sale and acquisition of businesses told me of a client who called him, saying, "We put the business up for sale, we have a buyer on the line, would you help us?" He helped by turning away the buyer, to the owner's dismay, prepping the business for sale as much as possible, and ultimately selling for one-third more than the initial offer.

Had the owners started three years before, their proceeds would have been millions more! My friend confirmed that this value differential is not at all unusual among mid-size businesses.

SPEED BUMP: Follow the five-year rule: If you might step back in five years, start conditioning the business immediately. It could be worth $2 million or more to you.

The 5-Step Business Conditioning System
Here are five steps to condition your business (yes, like conditioning your body). Like exercise, you won't get the reward without putting in the time. It takes at least three years; five years to be safe. Here's how.

Step 1: Keep It
Act like you'll keep it forever, regardless of whether you plan to sell. Your enemy is the dreamy escape from daily pressure. It leads to RHT, which is dreadfully expensive.

Step 2: Grow It
Decide to grow both revenue and profit by 25 percent in three years. Paint a picture of the business at 25 percent

24

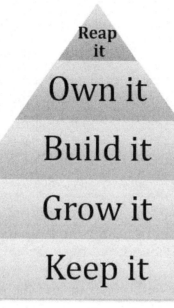

bigger, detailing at least these items:
• Sales
• Profit
• Number of employees
• Your income
• Investment needed

Insist on the first growth steps within 90 days by asking for the plan for that quarter. That plan will be the foundation for the one-year tactical plan and the three-year strategic plan that will scaffold your growth. Insist on both plan and action regardless of short-term noise in the business. Your life is at stake here.

Step 3: Build It
Boldly build the leadership team to deliver the growth and profit:
• Picture the team (position and skills) when sales are $25

million and growing. Paint this team together with your top leaders and advisors so that they see how things will look in numbers and leaders.

• Detail the first steps toward the picture, and begin in 14 days or less. Those steps will include training, hiring, and some demotions and turnover before you reach your goal.

• Build a leadership team that can grow the business better than you could, but with your values, drive, and pride.

• List the 10 most critical things you do, and systematically teach your new leader or leadership team to do them under your coaching. Then let go.

• Revisit the picture — the progress and the problems — every month with the team. Do this in spite of immediate business needs.

Step 4: Own It
Picture yourself as an owner, not as an owner-manager. Be the owner-investor you've wanted to be, without the daily dust-ups. Spell out your 12 personal quarterly steps from today to owner, stepping back as the business grows.

Step 5: Reap It
Your radical approach can deliver this triple pay boost:
• Keep your current income longer.

• Grow business value and get more when you sell.

• Raise your investment income when you sell.

Here's an example, which assumes profit growth of 25 percent in three years:

	This Year	**Three Years**
EBITDA	$1,200,000	$1,600,000
Market Multiplier	5X	5X
Sales Price	$6,000,000	$8,000,000
Investment Income @3%	$108,000/yr	$144,000/yr

Once at sale:
- Sale proceeds (pre-tax) $2,000,000
- 3 years of your current income $ 600,000
- Annually (investment income) $ 36,000

Cash difference: $2,600,000 + $36,000/year

ACCELERANT: What will you do with an extra $2 million?

SECRET BONUS: You can keep the business and own rising income and value.

Chapter 6
Harvest or Grow

Today we face a rare chance that has room for both prudence and opportunity: the best guess is that we're in early stages of a 10-year economic recovery. That economic strength argues powerfully for a special push to grow, in the face of attractive opportunities to harvest the current value of your business. Here's what that means:
• The next six years will provide one of the best opportunities in the past 50 years.
• The confluence of positive economic activity cuts risk dramatically.
• If you wait, you glide into the next recession, in about seven years.

Support for economic growth is shifting from government (interest rates will rise) to a stronger economy, marked by these changes:
• Increasing use of credit by business and households = spending.
• Stronger household confidence marked by rising wages, falling unemployment, low inflation, more job security (faster job growth and fewer layoffs), and low current consumer debt.
• Increased capital spending by business. Historically as capacity utilization approaches 80 percent, capital spending

spikes. Capacity utilization is now 79.6 percent and rising.

SPEED BUMP: This six-year runway will likely be the best chance for growing your business and your personal wealth in this lifetime.

What will speed you down the runway?
• Change your focus to valuation, not revenue or profit growth.
• Move from harvesting profit to investing in sharply higher valuation.
• Create company-wide enthusiasm for the thrill of building meaning.

Change Your Focus to Valuation
Valuation is what your business is worth, whether you sell it or keep it. It's calculated by this formula: EBITDA x Market Risk Multiple.

EBITDA is earnings before interest, tax, depreciation and amortization. Your accountant can show you how to pull the factors from your P&L and balance sheet, or call me.

Market Risk Multiple estimates the future earnings potential of your business. It ranges between 2 and 10. To estimate valuation, use a multiple of 4–6.

Application: If you can increase profit (actually EBITDA) about 25 percent in three years, the valuation increase ranges from $1 million to $3 million. Using a conservative multiplier of four, here's the math:
• Three-year EBITDA growth: $300,000 Valuation Growth: $1.2 million
• Three-year EBITDA growth: $500,000 Valuation Growth: $2 million

The valuation growth is real money, with benefits like these:
• If the business sells, it's extra money for the owners.
• If the owners keep the business:
 - There is greater company resilience to weather tough times.
 - Growth capital is cheaper and easier to obtain.
 - Better tools and toys are available to employees.
 - Top talent will be easier to retain or to attract.
 - Owner-managers can become owner-investors.
 - Most employees who want personal growth have that opportunity.

Move from Harvesting Profit to Investing in Sharply Higher Valuation

A common legacy of the 2010 recession is to keep doing what worked. That's harvesting profit, and it has already served its purpose. Instead, raise your head to look two years into the future, and ask these questions to change the trajectory of your company:
• How do I want my business to look in 24 months?
• What one accomplishment will boost our valuation dramatically?
• Who can help us accelerate it?

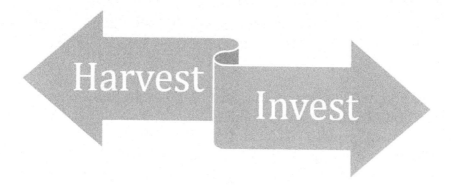

The Other Side of Succession

SPEED BUMP: Trajectory change is done by people, not analysis.

One of my clients struggled with a production manager who couldn't keep up with both growth and moving to a new building. On-time shipments dropped from 92 percent to 72 percent—a catastrophic cash bleed for a parts maker whose customers relied on timely delivery to ship their parts. The question wasn't whether to move out the production manager, it was where to find a competent replacement quickly enough. When we dug into organization reality with five old hands, they quickly found the formula for success: Move the swing shift manager to production manager, with a public agreement from the five that they would help him be successful.

On-time delivery, cash, and profit returned to normal levels in under three months.

Create Enthusiasm for the Thrill of Building Meaning
A growing organization can become a place of deep meaning for most employees. It's most powerful when it's beyond the product, looking also at personal growth, relationships, the thrill of achievement, and personal recognition. Strangely, good metrics can supply a foundation for all four, if their application moves past calculation to encouraging change.

The processes of change in a carefully paced, supportive environment can work like this:
• Personal growth: What can I do differently?
• Relationships: Look at what we accomplished!
• Achievement: We made progress toward our goal.
• Recognition: Thank you for stepping up. You kicked us forward!

ACCELERANT: Where will you multiply your valuation growth this week?

Chapter 7
Payoff Planning

There's confusion about where valuation fits in daily operation of a privately held business. Here's the answer:

SPEED BUMP: Measure profit until it's consistent, then measure valuation.

Okay, some explanation. Here are the three power paths to success:

Profit

Like all clichés, it's partly true. Actually you always measure profit, but you may change how it's viewed and applied. In addition to tracking net profit monthly and annually, most folks also watch net worth. Both are useful for operating day to day, but neither has much to do with the real valuation of your business. So what to do?

Until you're consistently profitable, profit is the monthly measure of progress, success, and motivation. No change there. Once you're consistently profitable, shift the light to valuation. Consistently profitable means five out of six months, with no major sign of abrupt change.

Think of profit as the cheap seats: You need it to get into the game, but it's a lousy value. It biases you against the risk that will make you successful, and it forces short-term leadership. It's necessary to pick up speed, but wasteful thereafter.

Valuation

Once you're profitable, build quickly on what you have. Your competitors are sprinting toward your niche and your customers, and unless you invest wisely and aggressively they'll beat you.

Valuation tracks the strength of your business in the market, including profit, growth potential, niche strength, management capability, ability to grow as needed, and so forth. It places your business in full context with your markets, your suppliers, and your competitors. Because valuation is broader than just a financial measure, it's reality on steroids. But these steroids are good for you, if you'll use them.

Valuation can be estimated well enough to provide power-ful guidance. Valuation's three elements are profit, EBITDA, and market multiple.
• Profit is your monthly summary of results as framed by your income statement.
• EBITDA is self-defining, and should be part of monthly financial reports (earnings before interest, taxes, depreciation, and amortization).
• Market multiple is an informed estimate of the risk of future profitability. Risk estimation is a critical skill when you sell, but your estimate will suffice for growth planning. For most planning, a multiple of 4 will suffice, even if you believe your company multiple will be different.

A sample calculation of valuation:
Annual Profit: $1,000,000
EBITDA: $1,200,000
Multiple: 4
Valuation: $4,800,000 (Multiple x EBITDA)

Investment
Once we're profitable, we've just entered the game. Much of the outcome depends on clever investment. Investments take many forms (people, information, equipment, marketing, etc.), but their purpose is to drive valuation.

Here's the investment trap: Imagine a $3.5 million investment. It seems promising, so bring on the ROI to help decide whether to move on it. How you calculate the "R" often determines whether you'll move or not.

The risk is that when your return ("R") seems too low, you'll skip the investment, and drift behind in the game.

The Other Side of Succession

Here's the math:

- Annual Profit: $1,000,000
- EBITDA: $1,200,000
- Multiple: 4
- Valuation: $4,800,000

Evaluate the opportunity:

Formula for ROI: Return/Investment
- Profit: $1,000,000 /$3,500,000 = 28.6%
- Valuation: $4,800,000/$3,500,000 = 137%

Bonus measure: Return Of Investment (Value of time)
- Profit: $3,500,000/$1,000,000 = 3.5 years
- Valuation: $3,500,000/$4,800,000 = .73 years

SPEED BUMP: Money sooner is better than money later; speed matters.

No, this isn't a shortcut. It's the actual return, because every major investment should be building your valuation. Period.

For most private businesses, the difference between 3.5 and .7 years is the difference between action and losing sleep (and rewards!). Of course time is money, but the real race is with your competitors, to serve current customers and gain new customers as soon as possible, while their need will make your offering most attractive. In a smaller way, the longer growth takes, the more it costs in interest expense on working capital, and there is the rising risk of market share loss. Time directly affects profit, which affects valuation, which impacts your return whether you sell or keep your business.

SPEED BUMP: Measure investments against valuation, not profit.

ACCELERANT: What is your valuation goal in 48 months?

Chapter 8
Grow Profit as Sales Slow

Early indicators suggest a possible slowing in the industrial sector of the economy (wait, this isn't an economic sleep-fest!), which could drag down sales growth for many — including you! Never mind the reasons. The question for you, as CEO, is "What do I do now?" Most of the time, most of us wait too long and then regret it.

Even worse, if you're looking at a potential change in ownership in the next five years, now's your chance to demonstrate the profit-making power of your business. Here's how: Instead of goosing sales in this hot market, harvest that emphasis, let sales continue to grow, but gently move your team to a better place: margin growth.

In the seven quarters that Mary Barra has been CEO at General Motors, sales have remained virtually flat at $40 billion, but adjusted EBIT has jumped from $500,000,000 to $3,000,000,000. Yes, that's billion — an increase of six times! But wait, there's more: You're thinking that GM was such a slug that just firing the laggards would produce this result. While that happened, it wasn't the driver (sorry, couldn't resist) of dramatic results. Instead, "To deliver those margins you've got to make the right decisions and look at yourself and say, 'Do I have a viable business [in a region or vehicle

The Other Side of Succession

segment]?' If I don't, I have no business being there."*

SPEED BUMP: Targeting will leverage profit quickly.

Here's how you can General Motors your way to better profit:

Eject Business Segments or Products with Little Hope of Profit
Once sales are moving, as they are for most of us, it's easy to overlook weak business segments. The blowback from disappointed customers or internal leaders can dilute leadership resolve. Vague benefits seldom trigger action, and by themselves each little segment may not promise enough to invest in change. If you target relentless margin improvement overall, the math can compel action. What is the impact on your operating earnings of a 1 percent increase in operating margin percentage?

Here's an example:

	Now	Then
Sales	$100,000,000	$100,000,000
Profit %	.6	.7
Profit $	$6,000,000	$7,000,000

SPEED BUMP: Increases in profitability can be powerful and quick.

Ignore Cost Accounting
Conventional wisdom requires that we improve our cost accounting to know where we're making money. That's almost always the wrong approach.

* Wall Street Journal, 10/26/15, p. R2

42

Jim Grew

Instead, charge your best minds with this three-step approach:

1. Target the weakest profit segments of the business. Remove allocations of overhead from your analysis until the end.

2. Ask them to estimate the biggest contributors of cost for the segment. Then reluctantly ask your financial team to sharpen the estimates of the top cost drivers in the segments targeted to go out the door. It's not perfect, but it pops out the answer. Refining the analysis won't change the action: Keep it or drop it.

3. As to overhead, once you've targeted a segment, mark the overhead costs for that business and remove them. If the costs aren't clearly tied to the product, ignore them. If the costs include people who are contributing to other products, challenge their manager to boost their performance.

Raise Prices
Invest in small but regular price increases, usually annually.

Instead of a 6 percent price boost in one jump, gentle prices up by 2 percent a year. Slow and steady won't attract attention for all but a few products.

Test the water on the sensitive ones with a 1 percent increase. You'll be surprised at the modest response. If there's a firestorm, leave the price alone and use the discussion to find other value to deliver to the customer. It's always there, if you look.

BONUS TIP: Skip the cuts to overhead. It delivers pennies, instead of the dollars you need.

ACCELERANT: Which business segments will you drop this quarter?

Chapter 9
A Valuable Partner

You definitely need some partners on this journey to succession, and your banker should not be overlooked in that capacity. Since your banker is your biggest investor, wouldn't he want you to thrive? Sadly, the more common picture of a banker is a narrow, grim money lender, full of limits and dumb questions. In fact, your banker is another asset (I know, bad pun) for your success, if you'll use him.

There are three reasons why your banker wants your success, beyond repaying your loan:

Reason 1 — Risk: As a senior executive of a major regional bank said, "My job is to manage risk." Yes, that's the risk to the bank that you won't repay your loan. But here's more: management is the shrewd balance of the pillars of business success: investment, market niche, and execution.

Investment is growth fuel, buying these growth engines:
• People
• Training
• Equipment
• Market penetration
• New products

Winners find their algorithm to balance the payoff and risk of each. Bankers can help find and maintain the success formula, if you'll let them.

Market niche: The "who" and "why" that is the doorway to powerful growth. The challenge here is to find the gold with the least pyrite and chase it hard.
• Who: The most common error is to chase a buyer who can't play. Qualifying may be more vital than prospecting, since it must include the customer's buyers.
• Why: Sales leaders use lead titration to clean the pipeline of buyers whose reasons to purchase will disqualify them at check-writing time.

Execution: Pride and fear can corrupt mid-level leaders as they chase results. Top-level leaders can dilute this corruption by fiercely testing for reality and nudging their leaders toward the most likely success paths. Their ability to aim enthusiasm toward reality will encourage their teams to give it their all.

USA women's soccer star Abby Wambach has built a legend from toughness and careful choices on the field. Her 183 career goals in international play beats Pele and Mia Hamm. Her discipline built those results on practice and great personal gifts, topped with thoughtful guidance on the spot for her teammates.

SPEED BUMP: Why not see how good your banker's advice might be?

Reason 2—Growth. Like you, your banker's company growth builds on successful current business. Every successful loan relationship enables another, sooner. Banks manage their loan portfolios like you manage your customers

46

(or should). That management is a mix of individual success and building the capacity to reach out for more. Sadly, we're more aware of the pain of recession's limits than we are of the exhilaration of growth in a strong economy. Both the pain and the exhilaration are the fabric of the banker's world, driving the search for successful relationships. All the reasons that you want growth will apply to your banker, so she's actually looking through the same viewer that you are.

SPEED BUMP: Did your last quarterly review look at possibilities, or only problems?

Reason 3 — Reputation. Just like you, reputation is the highest-leverage low-cost growth driver that there is. (Low current cost, of course. Reputation costs time, discipline, and patience for all of us.) Your bank's reputation can be a sales builder for you, if you'll seek it. They have more sales folks than you do, and they'd love to brag about you as a select

Every succession requires cash, for one of these purposes:
1. Provide buy-out funds to the current owner.
2. Fund the new leader or leadership team.
3. Provide capital investment to fund growth.

Usually current assets in the company aren't adequate to fund these and maintain current operations. Often the cheapest and fastest source of funds is your current banker, who has a big stake in your continuing success.

ACCELERANT: What will you ask from your banker this quarter?

Part 3 Leading the Way

Chapter 10
Habits of Compromised Companies

Recently I led a "Leading Change" workshop for clinical directors of a large and successful group of physical therapy clinics. Dramatic cuts in insurance payments have threatened their survival. Patient treatment hasn't changed, but most other clinic activity needs slimming down and speeding up.

This matters because most of the clinic directors are therapists who are part-time leaders, maintaining established procedures in their operation. When their job moved from "maintain" to "change," and that change involved their clinic team, they sought new leadership skills and help in using them. Leadership is now a vital part of their job, and without it they cannot remain as clinic directors.

SPEED BUMP: Some of your habits are outworn, potentially limiting future success.

The cliché "If it ain't broke, don't fix it" is as dangerous as it is comfortable. How can it square with the swirling change in our daily lives, and in our businesses? And yet I see organizations repeating processes that are inadequate, using techniques that are familiar but misguided, and applying advice from leaders and experts who haven't kept up. Devotion to this cliché will not see you successfully through your succession — or through any significant change.

It's not just about change in customers, products, and processes. It's making the adjustments that add value to the business — whether that means insulating it from damaging errors, or preparing it for a capital infusion as part of a sale, merger, or family succession.

Here's a hidden habit that is likely holding you back: your professional advisors and current and future leaders. Habit and relationship are vital lubricants for efficient application of skills to you and your business. Yet habit can block the hard-headed look at whether your leaders and advisors have kept up with you, your business, and your future.

Check your power triangle for current skills and processes. Power triangle?

Professional Advisors
A banker, insurance broker, attorney, accounting firm, investment manager, and an employee benefits managers

can all help reduce risk and speed growth if their expertise fits your need. Successful businesses grow with their expert advisors, for two reasons:

1. Business growth generates different risks and problems.
2. The skill mix of experts varies, because of experience, training, and interest.

Here's a simple way to be sure your advisors keep up: Ask them to prepare a review and update of your business situation. Do it at least every two years. They should do it gratis, as part of their continuing relationship with you. If they find a substantial need, even if it's costly, you're better off knowing about it. You can always delay or ignore it, which is better than letting it blindside you.

SPEED BUMP: To limit your personal risk as CEO, your personal advisors also must keep up with your changing situation.

Current Top Leaders
Midsize businesses especially struggle with reviewing and upgrading their executive teams. Finding and building an effective group of leaders is risky and tough, and that work diverts a busy CEO from the balance of daily reactions and active leadership for the future. The pressure to leave it alone is powerfully invisible.

I've noticed many successful companies that strapped everything down in 2009 to weather the recession haven't gone back outside to take a look at whether they are well equipped to harvest the bounty of opportunity now surrounding them.

Even tougher, it almost always requires outside eyes to see

real opportunity in the intersection of the present economy with a business leadership team.

Future Leaders

A recent discussion with a benefits expert exposed what may be the biggest weakness in midsize businesses: its future leaders. I have yet to meet a business with sales below $500,000,000 that has designated a replacement (or two) for each of its top five leaders; let alone implement the intensive development required for them to step into the senior position when it's time. What prevents it:

• The flood of reactive leadership that daily success demands.
• No urgency about a vague future possibility.
• Overwhelmed feelings about the opaque path to effective development.

SPEED BUMP: The comfortable flood of today is sabotaging your future.

THE TIME BOMB: Every business will change leaders, and likely will change owners. Those changes are like the side view mirror: we know that "objects in mirror are closer than they appear," and the wearying challenge of addressing them is beyond most leaders' bandwidth. Their very vagueness makes them dangerous, because their appearance is so hard to predict, and their effect is impossibly powerful.

ACCELERANT: Who is on your review calendar for this year?

Chapter 11
Repot or Shrivel

A huge Douglas fir tree in Portland's Rose Garden Park has divided itself into three trees about 30 feet up from its base. The "parent" trunk is three feet across; the "kid" trunks, springing from the base, are each about a foot in diameter. The vigor of this tree is the best image of successful succession I've seen yet.

But first let's clear the air about succession. Somehow it's come to mean a leader leaving his post. Like most clichés it's true enough, but stunningly limited. Succession can be about growing, not just about leaving or dying, and it's a staple of every successful leader and organization I've known. It hides under the rubric of "Change Management," but with richer context. If you'll repurpose the word to mean personal growth and enhanced impact, you'll re-energize yourself and your firm like the tree.

A remarkable number of CEOs and owners that I've known have admitted that they're bored. I'm prescribing Succession: take one daily, and don't leave your firm. You'll love the person you become.

SPEED BUMP: Delegation is the single best preparation for succession.

The Other Side of Succession

Delegate early and often. Here's what it can get you:

• A continually energized and growing firm.
• A jump in management bandwidth that can conquer top opportunities.
• Vision so clear that reality and opportunity leap into sight.

A Continually Energized and Growing Firm
Jewel Food Stores dominated the grocery business in Chicago for decades. Its 25 percent market share was unheard of in a major metropolitan area. It focused relentlessly on finding and developing talented people, promoting them to key leadership positions in their late 20s and early 30s. It developed a "Skunk Works" separate chain of stores called The Outer Zone, located in a ring about 40 to 70 miles outside Chicago. This was where most new initiatives were tested (and often developed) before rollout in the city. This is where young leaders were developed and proven, with real profit responsibility.

The process of delegating forces a leader to hire and grow competent leaders. No one hands the ball to folks who can't learn to use it well. The impact on hiring and training gets new urgency, instead of languishing by the roadside like many "HR" initiatives. Let's face it: There are few things as energizing as trying to start your car as it sits in the crossing with a train bearing down. New responsibilities are like that train, you know.

A Jump in Management Bandwidth That Can Conquer Top Opportunities
More skilled players are likely not only to deliver better results sooner, but their drive will pull the business into opportunities that now swim by unnoticed. There is a reason that world-class sailboats have a crew: the captain couldn't

sail without them, let alone win.

Vision So Clear That Reality and Opportunity Leap into Sight
Yes, the "Vision Thing" is overblown, but here's the opportunity: Real leaders point to the next real opportunity like Sacajawea pointed to the next mountain for Lewis and Clark. Your explorers need you to help them see the great opportunities and pass up low-payoff iterations of the present. If no one is looking, what will you miss?

Weightless Weight Lifting
Here's how a powerful leader who delegates and sees can carry a vigorously successful organization (without feeling the weight).

Intel recently hired a Chief Marketing Officer from Staples. It's unprecedented for a deeply engineering-driven firm to look outside for a powerful vision of customer possibilities. In fact, it's 180 degrees from the core that built the company: *Engineer Moore's Law into better and better products. Customers will see the benefits and throng to buy them.* Brilliant engineering design is still producing chips that meet Moore's impossible standard, but the vital shift is about a new path to customers.

One of my early mentors, the chairman of a $7 billion firm, told me that he tried to "repot" himself every five to seven years. I watched him do it, replacing himself twice as he moved up and onto the board of directors. His company was dominant in its markets for decades.

Why repot yourself? That's the wrong question. As life happens to us, we repot, or are repotted. So the real question is, "Do you want to be the potter, or be potted?" You've been a decision maker about your business to this point; why change now?

ACCELERATOR: Do you have the guts to "repot" yourself?

Chapter 12
Through the Delegation Doorway

We often do one thing in theory, and something entirely different in practice. As leaders we may know it's more about our people than it is about us, but in practice it is quite another story. The hardest leadership lesson to stick to is that it's not about what you do, it's about what your people do. Delegation is the doorway to succession.

Intellectual understanding of delegation is not enough of course. Go with your gut, and then go with action. Here are clues signaling that you may still be thinking that leadership is about you:
• You work hard on managing your time.
• You work hard on all of your communications to your people.
• You come to tactical planning sessions with goals already written out.
• You master the numbers.
• You "let your managers manage."
• You avoid checking on how things are going, because it's upsetting to see your unrealized dreams all around you.
• You really think that you know better than your people do.
• You haven't read a novel or seen a play for more than a year.

The Other Side of Succession

• Your advisors are comfortably familiar, and you're choosy about what you take to heart.
• You try hard to do things well.

Each of those is more curse than blessing. And if this is you, there are some steps to take as you make the mental (and real) leap to succession planning. As an antidote, I suggest you try these powerful reversals:

• Work on your priorities for FIVE minutes a day, and the rest on your leaders' choice of priorities.
• Listen more, talk less. You'll be shocked at what your people will discover with you.
• Come to planning sessions centered and comfortable with your team's competence.
• Charge someone else with predigesting the numbers for you, and show them how.
• Ask your managers what they need.
• Go see every day what's going on in your organization. Look everywhere.
• Get over yourself. Your job is to enable your people to know more than you do, and act on it.
• Expand your mind outside your business, with the same drive that you put into your success.

A lighthouse is often squat and plain, and close up it doesn't look equal to its task. "But," as Farnham Street blogger Shane Parrish said, "it isn't the lighthouse that matters. It's the light."

Are you so busy with yourself that your light is dim?

Here's an example of light that you can apply right now*. It's from Regina Dugan, head of Google's ATAP unit (Advanced Technology and Projects), who describes her team as "a small band of pirates trying to do epic s**t." Dugan is fresh from three years as head of DARPA, the legendary Defense Department research group that in fact invented the Internet, GPS, and stealth aircraft, among others. Dugan's team uses one of these two approaches to make huge leaps:

• Observe where technology is heading, and accelerate it.
• Find an application that needs a new type of technological solution.

Here's your version to jump-start improved performance in your teams:
• See where attempts at improvement are working, and speed them up.
• Spot an exciting outcome that could be within reach, and charge your best folks with jumping to conclusions until they find a way that works.

Here's a leadership tip from Sesame Street that can boost the performance of your leaders now and into the future**: Sesame Street's first guest star, James Earl Jones, recited the alphabet in 1969 in his characteristic slow, sonorous voice. The trick: Jones stopped after each letter, leaving space for kids to say the next letter. Apply these leadership-building techniques as part of your succession planning:

Your version: Ask the first question, and wait, wait, wait, wait for your people to try out an answer. Reinforce it, and wait again. They'll see that you know they can do it, and they will. (The little help they'll need will come easily to you and will leave them with the thrill of leading the charge.)

Watch yourself: Are you so busy being the lighthouse that there's no light? That's a sure way for your projects and goals to crash against the rocks. Be the light, and let your

The Other Side of Succession

people captain their own ships.

What's this have to do with your succession? These are the people who will help keep your business growing even as you slow down.

* Fortune, September 1, 2014   ** "Sesame Street," Parade, User

Chapter 13
Procrastination — Friend or Enemy?

If you're a successful leader, you procrastinate. The issue is that it's often prudent, sometimes harmless, and occasionally disastrous. The trick is not to stop procrastinating (not possible), but to choose it as a leadership skill — particularly as you are looking toward succession.

Procrastination has a bad rap. Regardless of whether we're perfectionists or impulsives, we likely procrastinate and hide self-criticism of it with either blame or impassive ignorance.

Instead of hiding, consider the latest facts:
1. Everyone procrastinates.
2. It's necessary for high-functioning health.
3. It's risky behavior.

The CliffsNotes version is that emotional self-regulation is essential for successful leaders, and procrastination is a useful tool in the self-regulation toolbox. It's a way to let off pressure, make space for others in the problem-solving process, and allow the right (creative) side of your brain to wander in search of a better solution. Wandering is essential food for creative thought, critical when obstacles block known avenues of progress. As an added benefit, it can also make room for effective delegation.

The Other Side of Succession

Procrastination includes an emotional "payoff" that's different for different folks. It's replacing a desirable activity with a short-term pleasure.

Which of these is your payoff of choice, when you procrastinate?
1. Doing something that's good (healthy, generous, kind) — for example, going to the gym.
2. Doing something useful, but not the task at hand.
3. Doing anything else that's popped up and looks interesting.
4. Doing something that takes your mind off bad feelings — for example, eating.

Leadership Payoffs for Procrastination:
• It can shift problems from leader to team. Winning teams take most problems away from their leaders and solve them, seeking help when they are stumped. This is an economical use of a leader's skill and time, and multiplies her impact on the organization.

• It creates space for others to solve the problem on their own initiative, which provides deep satisfaction to most folks. It's also a powerful growth tool that takes little leadership time, unlike most training which requires more time from the leader.

• It morphs the problem in a good way. With time, the current problem often changes into one of two better forms, accelerating a solution:
     - Dissolved into nothing.
     - A clearer problem that's easier to solve.

Here's how problems get better with procrastination:

For the leader who is anxious and impulsive, procrastination is a special blessing. It replaces low-value targets with the higher-payoff targets that appear with time. Instead of jumping to solve the problem at hand, waiting usually enables a better solution that is:
• Faster
• Cheaper
• Higher impact

SPEED BUMP: Procrastination is actually an acceleration technique.

SPEED BUMP WARNING: Some procrastination costs more than its benefit.

These high-cost procrastinations usually are the fruit of anxious impulsiveness in the face of turtle-speed progress. All leaders encounter this. Since impulsiveness is one of the two prime drivers of procrastination, observe your impulsiveness and delay action for a better solution.* This can be harder than it looks, since there's a fine line dividing impulsiveness and action orientation. This simple answer works most of the time: When it's a hot question, slow down, ask questions, and wait a bit. Let it come to you. Your creative brain emerges when your impulsive brain hits a wall, so put up a temporary wall for better results.

The Other Side of Succession

Transitioning out of your business is a big, unfamiliar, risky, and complex decision. It's made for healthy procrastination. However, to avoid the hiding that boosts your risk of a bad outcome, start down the planning road immediately. Planning is cheap, can be changed, and is essential to a good outcome. Then a bit of procrastination can lead to a payoff.

ACCELERANT: What will you put off today?

* Wall Street Journal, September 1, 2015, p. D1

Chapter 14
Surgical Leadership

Remarkably, most succession discussions leave leadership development to the last, after taxes, estate plans and legal structures. Yet it's the successful transition to future strong leaders that determines whether cash flow will fund the desired future successfully.

In 2015 the Golden State Warriors became the first San Francisco team to bring home an NBA title since 1975. Their story is as much about management and leadership off the court as it is about the players and coaches.

Six months after Silicon Valley veteran venture capitalist Joe Lacob bought the team in 2011, he upgraded both discipline and talent in the senior management group, to put it mildly.

Their performance was on display every game night. Of course they have gifted players, Steve Kerr as coach, and a remarkable record. However, it wouldn't have happened without the leadership upgrade, according to owner Lacob. "You can attribute it to luck, or to the people we picked."*

Of course picking people is just part of the story; it's also about how the organization is led.

The Other Side of Succession

These leadership pillars mark winners:

The Right Leaders
Warriors owner Lacob says he's learned to "pick people" in working with 130 Silicon Valley firms. It's not just the picking, though that's vital. It's the willingness to make a space for the new and stronger leader by moving someone aside or creating a new position.

The challenges of a winning succession make picking and placing even more vital. Cost and habit are the enemies here, and because they're out of the limelight, they can generate damaging fog from their closets.

SPEED BUMP: Which of your top leaders can be moved to open the growth door?

Active Vision
Vision isn't gazing, it's finding the next action target. The difference compared to traditional vision is that it always includes action, but requires space to see and create. One of the companies where I worked has sales 30 percent ahead of two years ago, with profit coming along nicely. They roared out of the recession by re-casting their leadership team, pushing for the next growth step before the last steps were digested.

Here's what they did:
1. Carefully developed their best salesman by training him in project management and production before moving him to sales.
2. Invested nearly $1,000,000 in two highly focused process equipment upgrades in their manufacturing operations.
3. Considered and rejected many other appealing paths to profit growth.

They are now examining expansion to the east coast.

SPEED BUMP: Vision means little without timely action.

Move to the Marrow
Instead of trying to be "the decider," or letting your team make the decisions, move to the marrow of effective action. Most executives wallow between pleasing their boss and finding action paths with acceptably low risks.

The CEO who is looking to increase valuation and pave the way for the future (whatever that means to you in terms of succession) frames discussion, agendas, and "no's" to give his team a playing field where they can excel. That means blowing up agendas and activities that are small bore or off-target, regardless of their appeal. It also means creating spaces of no action, where thought and debate can safely occur.

If you think you do this well and regularly, ask your team this question: What's the top opportunity that we're missing? You may have to ask twice to get them to believe that you want their thought, not just their answer.

SPEED BUMP: Do you dally in discomfort, or do you lurch to decision in discomfort?

Your "warrior leadership" might look like this:

The Right Leaders → Active Vision → Move to the Marrow

ACCELERANT: Which of your leaders needs to move?

*San Francisco Chronicle, June 7, 2015, p. A1

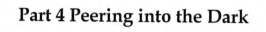

Part 4 Peering into the Dark

Chapter 15
What Is in Your Succession Darkroom?

I asked Larry, "What do you want to do?"

Larry answered, "I don't know what I want to do. I know I don't want to take it to zero."

Larry is in his sixties and a successful founder of a 35-year-old company, which is in its next surging growth cycle. Larry is a prototype of the many brightly successful founders I've met; they all find themselves mired in these realities, looking for a light:

Reality 1: Change Is Coming.
Larry knows that at some point his current business and life situations will change dramatically.

Reality 2: Advice Floods Don't Help.
The flood of advice from well-meaning advisors addresses the nits but not the substance. The nits are questions like these:
• What's your retirement financial plan?
• How will you sort out what your family gets?
• What is needed to make your business legally ready for changes in leadership?
• Is your tax-minimization plan current and powerful?

75

These are all the right questions, all in some stage of sorting as the British say, and all beside the point. Yes, they are vital. No, they are not the answer. They are braces and frames for Larry's house, but he hasn't designed the house yet.

SPEED BUMP: Retirement mechanics aren't the path to your next delight.

Reality 3: Not Zero.

Zero means full stop, dead in the water, going nowhere. This describes what to avoid but sheds no light on what to go for next. Larry is unprepared for the first time since he was a teen. The real life questions are not defensive, they are offensive. The defensive questions can be answered by his excellent advisors (see Advice Floods, above). Sadly, defense doesn't generate forward motion; it blocks action. It's necessary, but vastly incomplete.

Here's how the darkroom looks:

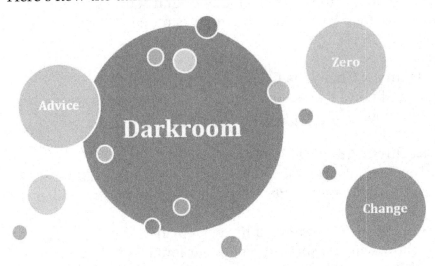

The Friendly Constraint Problem

Most business owners, in my experience, have long ago confined their life to a well-defined game: build and succeed in this business, or these businesses. The questions, challenges, and rewards are predictable, even though their solutions are perpetually maddening. Life decisions are defined by the questions, defined by the businesses, defined by the game.

SPEED BUMP: Questions limited to a specific game are simpler to answer.

The new question isn't how to win the game. It's not even which business game to enter. Instead, the question is how do I find a new game that has these characteristics?
• I will enjoy it.
• I can learn it in time to succeed well enough.
• It fits with the other parts of my new life.

SPEED BUMP: The new life game isn't buying, starting or building another business.

As Bing Crosby sang in the film classic *White Christmas*, "What can you do with a general when he stops being a general?" (Irving Berlin)

The answer is in the darkroom of the future, unlit and mysterious. It's dark because it asks different questions than most business owners expect, and answers come from new places. Strangely, the same people who've used relentless innovation and creativity to build their businesses find themselves bereft, fumbling for an answer to a question that seems to come from left field: What do I want to do?

ACCELERANT: What is your path to finding your new life game?

Chapter 16
Use a Bigger Shovel

Looking into your personal darkroom (how your future life will really be) may either be your nirvana (if you're a thinker) or your nemesis (if you'd rather just do something). This is not about which you are; it's a way to improve your future life regardless of how you're wired.

The fine line between confidence and success includes phases of accepting help in the dark spots. Real winners seek help in areas where they're already successful. For some reason this is common in athletics, and rare in business. Testosterone can't be the answer.

SPEED BUMP: Step around your resistance to powerful help; this is your big game.

One way to avoid help is to get wimpy help, so you can say you did. This takes the form of talking with your accountant or lawyer or financial advisor, who may be smart but doesn't have the skill to really get into what matters with you on this topic. If you're a wide receiver, you probably don't spend much time with the line coach. The test for a competent helper: Does he make you a bit anxious, on top of your absolute trust in him?

The Other Side of Succession

What's the bigger shovel? Do some serious digging into who you are, and accept the need for a bright light along the way. Miners wear a lamp to stay alive; the choices you're trying to unearth can be equally deadly if done wrong.

Here are some serious shovels:

Shovel 1: What If You're Rich?
Imagine that you have all the money you'll need to take care of your life and your family in ways that you desire. Now ask yourself:
• What would I change?
• How will I see my gifts with the courage to apply my personal power?
• What would get me off my chair?

Shovel 2: What If You'll Die in Five to Ten Years?
Since you won't have advance notice of your death:
• What will you do now?
• How will you bring it to life?
• When will you start?

Shovel 3: What If You'll Die Tomorrow?
This may be your doorway to richer answers to the above questions. What do you wish you'd done? (And please skip the Bucket List, which is a lazy way of avoiding careful thought.) Start with these three:
• Relationships
• Play
• Worthy causes

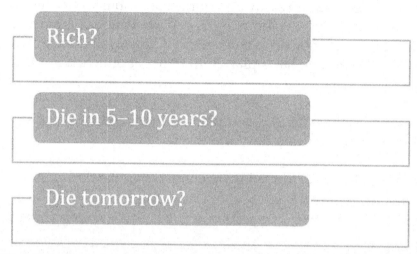

Here's how to bring the three questions to life:
1. Write each question at the top of its own page (type or handwrite, but do it.)
2. Do one page each day within a week.
3. Spend no more than 30 minutes on each page.
4. Calendar it like it is a payday.
5. Return to each page three times in three weeks to enrich your lists.
6. Rank each item on each page A, B, C in importance to you.
7. Pick the top A on each page.
8. Start on one A immediately after you've ranked the three pages.
9. Revisit your pages in one month. Update the rankings, and then review with your most powerful advisor. (Powerful means she cares about you, she knows you, she wants the best for you.)

SPEED BUMP: Actually doing this will be one of the hardest things you've done.

The power of an advisor is in accountability. While you may think you've been accountable to others for your business, these actions sweep away all your accountability structures. Your odds of success jump if you replace your accountability structure, and they drop below zero if you don't. Boxer Mike Tyson: "Everyone has a plan until they get punched in the face."

Test yourself: What did you plan to do today that you didn't do? How about yesterday, and the day before?

ACCELERANT: How will you come out of the darkness smiling?

Chapter 17
The Importance of Triggers

Each of us has many triggers, from road rage (that %!@#* in the other car) to the thousandth iteration of your spouse's unwelcome suggestion. And then there are the good ones, such as the power of a success, the thrill of the hunt for a new key employee, the dramatic product breakthrough that you're about to launch.

A trigger is an experience that causes you to change course, although a trigger is powerless in itself. Like the road rage driver, it's all about your reaction, not their behavior. When you bring to your darkroom the habits of waiting for triggers for action, the odds are good that you'll find either the wrong triggers, or none at all. "None at all" is evidence that you're out of practice at creating your own triggers. The problem is that the darkroom is dark: you can't see your future, and your usual tools need adapters to work in these conditions.

SPEED BUMP: Rebuild your trigger capability, or you'll stay stuck.

Why do triggers matter so much? Much of life is the same struggle in new clothes. A time management (oxymoron) staple is that 80 percent of a leader's time is already spo-

The Other Side of Succession

ken for, so impact demands careful use of the remaining 20 percent (that's one day a work week for those of us who live in the theory of things). Years of swimming in the 80 percent come with an unwelcome adaptation: most action comes from triggers. That can be good, except that most triggers come from outside us, and aren't our creation.

SPEED BUMP: Create your own triggers, or you'll be a prisoner in your own life.

The trigger problem is not about lack of imagination. You've fueled your business success with daily doses of imagination. That's what it's called when you pull a new solution either out of your brain or your team. It's a survival skill that you've proven.

The trigger problem is urgency, strangely enough. In your early days of leadership you created urgency out of desperation or desire, because there wasn't an alternative. As you've developed a successful business, momentum and success have redirected urgency to response. That means that the situation is created for you, by your business or customers or competitors or suppliers. Now you must become the creator of your own urgency if you want to break past habits and step out of the stream of today.

SPEED BUMP: Create urgency out of whole cloth instead of the current situation.

In a manufacturing company where I worked, we created urgency with a ridiculously simple bonus system. Since we shipped to order, we knew a month ahead what our shipments should be. Depending on projected sales, margins, and cash, we set a monthly bonus target of $50–$200. If we hit our shipment target with 100 percent quality, every employee got a check for that month's bonus amount. The power: They knew the goal. They tracked progress daily in a United-Way-type thermometer, and at the end of the month they knew immediately whether they'd won and how much they'd receive. It boosted profits by millions in a year!

Triggers are the engine that will get you to your next amazing future. Here are the core first steps. The secret is to repeat several times for triggers powerful enough to blow you into your future:

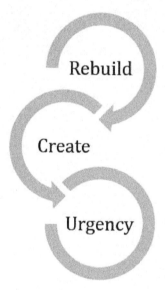

ACCELERANT: What's your urgency about your future?

Chapter 18
More Than Golf and Travel

"Everybody I know that's retired has died in less than five years," said the guy who is repotting himself after 40 years of successful business leadership. He's brought in a leader to gradually replace him, and he's finding himself at loose ends.

Make no mistake: He loves to travel, he plays golf with friends in the rain, and he looks forward to month-long odysseys in his RV with his wife. He's just as clear that all this plus his part-time role at his business just isn't "it."

Evidence: After we enjoyed meeting for the first time at a resort in Maui, he suggested that we get together when we returned home. His answer to the invitation was "I'm in your neighborhood almost every week. I'll drop by." Sounds like he's not fully in either retirement or leading his substantial business. (He's a blunt construction business leader, so he has no trouble saying no if that's what he wants.)

SPEED BUMP: There's more to your darkroom life than extending your past.

What's operating here is habit built on fear multiplied by aversion. If you flip it on its head, it's no clear path with no way to build one. What's in the way is that he's looking in the wrong direction. All his business life he's looked at his business as the prime driver of challenge and satisfaction. Even with its moments of terror separated by occasional joy and regular boredom, it was a golf kind of life. The joke is that all that it takes to bring a golfer back next week is one good shot on each nine.

Darkroom Formula:

Habit

Fear

Aversion

Dark

Boredom

SPEED BUMP: Moving out of your old job won't deliver the highs that moved you.

Think about it. The constant push-pull of business leadership is like a Western movie: good guys, bad guys, action, near-death experiences. Do you really think that someone who loved that life will thrive in a rocker?

The question is not what to do. It's how to find what to do when you're beyond rusty at it. Your "what to do" is about either growing a business, buying a business, or leading a business. If you remove "business" from that sentence, what's left is the search formula, in three parts. Here's how to start to light up your darkroom:

It's about You, Not the Business
• Stop looking at the business for a moment, and figure out where you are.
• Accept your blind spots, even though you can see them.
• Find at least two senior advisors who care about you, see you, and will question you. Let them question you vigorously about what lights you up. Listen carefully.

As I looked for my way after successful runs in two large corporations, I stumbled through two careers with mixed results. (Worked with a guy who was convicted of bank fraud; sold investment real estate until I was bored silly.) The lights came on when a friend spent an afternoon pouring beer into me and asking probing questions, until he opined, "You're a leader. Forget about being a corporate marketing guy." I've successfully improved 25 companies since then.

SPEED BUMP: Since you know it's hard to see yourself, get help.

Investor, Leader, or Do-er—Which Are You?
Here's the fog-cutter:
• Investors love analysis like they love poker or fantasy football. They don't want to get mud on them, and they'll take a loss from time to time, just to stay in the game.
• Leaders feed off the growth and accomplishments of people. Unless that feeds you deeply, it's not really you. Many business leaders love the puzzle but can't stand the drone of people issues.
• Do-ers either devised the concept that became their busi-

ness, or they live in their garage to rebuild cars or remodel their houses. These "tinkerers" are happiest when they're wrapped around their workbench.

Pick One and Try It

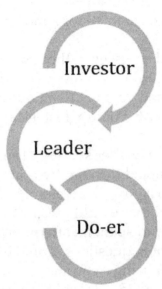

Investor

Leader

Do-er

Pick One and Try It
Investors will often stay in their business as investors instead of daily leaders. Their model is Board Chair, whether there is a board or not.

Leaders will find another organization to lead. The smartest ones will find either a business that fascinates them deeply, or they'll find a charity that they believe in from their heart. Either needs their skill, feeding their hope to fuel noteworthy success.

Do-ers will answer these questions:
• Looking back from age 12, what projects lit me up?
• What is within reach that's like the best of my past?
• What can I start this week?

ACCELERANT: What will you try this week?

Part 5 Looking to Legacy and Beyond

Chapter 19
Boost Your Legacy (Even if You're Wealthy, Wealth Matters)

Michael Jordan cried.

"A humbled and emotional Michael Jordan fought back tears, feeling vindicated after years of criticism, after being named the Charlotte Business Journal's Business Person of the Year." Here's more: "For all of the people that think that I'm in this for the short term, you better pull your socks up... because my promise to this organization and this community is to bring a winner," Jordan said. "I left home. I came back home. And I plan on staying home," North Carolina Native Jordan said.*

If you're still confused about what "legacy" might mean to you, read about Jordan again. What do you and Michael Jordan share? The shock of an unfinished legacy, which looks more like a scratch and dent sale than the sleek beauty that you imagined so recently.

SPEED BUMP: Legacy often trumps all other life achievements.

*AP, January 21, 2015

95

The Other Side of Succession

Doubt it? Take this 30-second quiz. Look at the list below:
1. Your kid
2. Your mom
3. Your dad
4. Your favorite employee
5. Your long-time customer
6. Your best friend

Pick the one you focused on first. How would it feel to lose that person?

The legacy reverse: Legacy is not how you feel about that person; it's how that person feels about you. It's how you are seen. And if this is too close to home, then it's how people feel about your business.

SPEED BUMP: The more you reject how you're seen, the bigger the blast when you move on.

Legacy is what you've built and what you've left in your wake. It's seldom considered until the "end" is in sight, when it's too late to do much about it. Succession often births this leadership triple whammy:

1. I'm losing a centerpiece of my life.
2. I can see my control slipping away.
3. Other people will assign my legacy to me.

SPEED BUMP: Your legacy will be defined by others unless you define it first.

Kick-start your legacy, and power it up now:

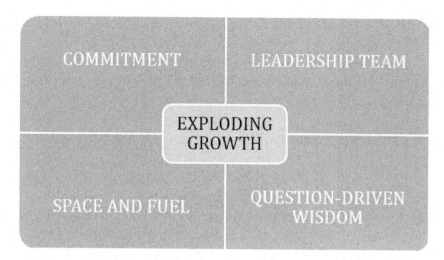

Seizing the Opportunity
The hidden gem in defining your legacy is the opportunity in front of you now. Exploiting that opportunity requires a shift in thinking that impacts your business now, and your legacy later. Here's how you do it:

1. Commit early, at least five years before the first possible succession step.
2. Shift your thinking from planning your exit to dramatic business growth.
3. Shift from what you'll get at succession to what you can give to your leaders and your organization.
4. Provide the space and the fuel (capital, hard questions, and praise) to enable your young leaders to blast through barriers to success.
5. Replace directives with questions designed to expose risk and find answers.
6. Invest the five years (minimum) it will take to build a successful leadership team.

Here's how to define a successful leadership team:
• The number of problems that come to me decline.

- The problems that get to me are more and more complex and sophisticated.
- Growth momentum in the company accelerates.
- I hand off most of the tasks that I had previously reserved for myself.

SPEED BUMP: You're at the top of your game. Why waste it?

One of my clients was a family business whose succession was well planned financially and legally. The parents' new roles seemed clear, but holes in their planning replaced the joy of legacy with pain and frustration as they watched their son struggle as CEO. The business seemed solid, but successor leadership was fragile and unformed — too weak to master the urgency of ownership. Instead, leadership power struggles nearly sunk the business, destroying an industry legend.

The remedy? We built a new leadership team with the CEO, developing practices that honored historic values and enhanced earnings and industry reputation. The same leadership succession planning could have started five years earlier, avoiding damage to profit, morale, and industry reputation.

ACCELERANT: What is your picture of your business legacy in five years?

Chapter 20
The Bridge to Your New Company

Are you over 50 and leading a company that's owned by
your family? Which fork in the road will you choose?
• Paint inside diminishing lines?
• Make your mark?

SPEED BUMP: The first trick is realizing that now is the
time.

This is not so simple, since your personal philosophy can
enable future success or drown the company in backwash
from the past. The tiresome legend of the controlling father
choking the child's dream is just true enough to survive, but
seldom describes reality in my experience. Instead, reality is
almost entirely in the successor's hands. But here's the rub:
the way dad starts the transition can either boost it to success or doom it to years of hopeful staggering. Which do you
want? Here's some perspective.

SPEED BUMP: The second trick is taking action now.

Nautor's Swan is a line of eye-popping sailing yachts, now
2000-strong worldwide. These Finnish "wind palaces" are
hopelessly expensive, combining smooth sailing in rough
seas with stunningly comfortable interiors. "It's more like

a floating sculpture than a sailboat." Deck planking is in a straight line, instead of curving like most luxury yachts. Besides being striking to look at, it avoids rope snarls, a racing sailor's nightmare. Every detail is designed and nearly all are built in Jakobstad, a Finnish town on the Gulf of Bothnia. This 50-year-old family business recently sold to another family business, Palazzo Feroni Finanziara S.P.A, led by Leonardo Ferragamo, one of the heirs of legendary shoemaker Salvatore Ferragamo.

Leonardo's take on family business succession:
"Heritage is the foundation for the bridge you want to build. You need to respect it, but not just maintain it...we want a stronger drive toward evolution—never revolution."*

SPEED BUMP: Your foundation isn't your future.

Here's an evolutionary framework to guide dad:

• Pour it into your successor's lap. Let your son or daughter take more than you think he or she can handle—lots more, sooner. Actually take yourself into your own past, when you were that age. You'll be shocked at what you were doing. It's not a bad template to use.

• Shift your senior leadership team to the future. Odds are that your "powerful" management team is effective because you're in it. Take this self-test: how confident would you be to leave for two months with no connection, including phone calls? The rub is that the skills that helped you build the company, and grow it from small to substantial, are out of date as developer of the management team of your future. A starter answer: treat them like your child (see above).

* Wall Street Journal, September, 2015, p 120

• Fly rod grip. Fly fishermen know that a light touch with the rod is the only way to lay a fly just upstream from that beautiful fish. The light touch enables the quick, sensitive reactions that success (and catching the fish) require. Try this at work!

| Pour it on | Leadership team for the future | Fly rod grip |

ACCELERANT: How will you frame the evolution of your company?

The Bridge

26

Chapter 21
Stepping Back without Stepping in It

I recently talked with a founder whose son is doing a good job of running the company, but not at the level that dad wants. While we found some good ways for him to help his son, the clumsiness was apparent. He imagines himself as chairman; his son sees him as dad first, chairman second. Pleasing dad trumps dramatic business leadership for son, diluting both talent and results. They're back to driver's ed, with dad punching the floor to stop, diverting son from driving safely.

SPEED BUMP: Neither son nor dad is ready for dad to step back, but here they are.

The problem is not that dad doesn't know better. Rather, he assumes that he can make it work in spite of what others have done. Some call that hubris; others may label it as bad judgment. The stick in his spokes is the strong family feelings that he and son share. Skiers call it "out over your tips."

SPEED BUMP: Accept that you're underprepared to step back, and prepare.

What can you do?

The Other Side of Succession

Here is the gold standard, beyond having first-rate advisors:

1. Enhance sustained future cash flow in the business.
Since cash flow comes from excellent management, how will you replace yourself? Skip the modesty, since likely you've built a leadership group that relies on you for final support, regardless. Here's the trade-off: if you decide you can't afford a first-rate replacement, you likely have hobbled the cash machine you've built. That cash shortfall affects employees and owners, who often are your family. It funds their lives, your retirement, and the business's future. Even though you had it working smoothly, it wasn't automatic (why did you spend so much time at work, if you weren't needed?), and entropy can dilute it quickly.

2. Include key family members in planning five years before you step back. Most of your family have feelings about the business regardless of their role in it. Whether they are supported by it, see a personal growth opportunity in it, or want to "put their mark on it," they need as much time and space as you do to find both a suitable path to change and a winning landing spot. As one of my clients said, "I realized that I'm the same age my dad was when he started the business, and I want to put my mark on it." Powerful feelings at work.

3. Choose the business over your family. As you start working on your new role, and the future roles of family members in the business, put the business first. That means that as you evaluate answers to all the questions about family involvement, start with "What does the business need?" Then ask how your family members can enable future business success, not the other way around. Of course you can't know for sure how your family will do as leaders, but use your years of hiring experience to make the best judgments

106

possible. For instance, it's admirable to promote a daughter with the proviso that she lean into developing her skills in the two areas that need it. You help by identifying the training need, and supporting the company investment in that.

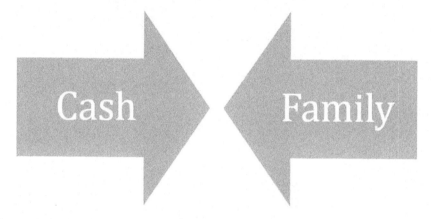

ACCELERANT: When is your first real family discussion about your future?

Chapter 22
Watching Dad Isn't Enough

As you read this, family businesses all over the country are on a hopeless quest. The path is unmarked, the territory is new, and the goal is barely achievable. That quest is to help daughter or son to become the next successful CEO of the business.

Not only are the odds of success lousy, but the cost of failure is a stunning series of frustrations, disappointments, and losses—and that's before the financial and emotional costs. Full disclosure: This is not a screed about the progressive weakness of each generation. That tired trope is of dubious credibility, and of no value in this discussion.

Each family operates in its unique situation, and generalizations require adaptation to reality to be useful. A common abuse of medical studies is to apply study results to an individual case, even though the data describes outcomes and probabilities for a group, not an individual. The point: it is useful to know the odds, but not sufficient. Evidence? Thousands flock to casinos expecting to be just special enough to beat the well-known odds against them. Our desire to be special is a requirement for a successful life, but it's a barrier to embracing our realities as insufficient teachers for our daughters or sons.

The Other Side of Succession

SPEED BUMP: Even though my kid is special, that's not enough for success.

Do you know anyone who has learned to ride a bike or a skateboard by watching others? Watching others helps with some details, of course. But ask yourself: Do your golf skills improve by watching the golf channel? Your enthusiasm may get a boost, but until you go to the driving range your skills won't step up, not even a bit. And even that's not enough to really improve your game. What's missing? The teacher.

SPEED BUMP: Being a successful CEO doesn't mean I can teach it to my kid.

Here's why it's so hard for a parent to grow a kid into a successful CEO:

It's harder because it's your kid. The relationship requires dad to shift from what he thinks is right to the intersection of what his kid wants to learn and what future success demands. The relationship is charged. For example, the kid wants to please and be independent at the same time, while the dad wants the kid to do what he thinks will benefit the kid while enabling what looks like potential failure. Successfully living in this dynamic for years is beyond the reach of most folks, even with the best motives.

SPEED BUMP: Dad must shift from an object of approval to a resource.

This shift happens in the kid's mind, and there's little a parent can do to make it happen. Enable, possibly. The kid must do it through experiencing her own success, failure, and resilience to build her own sense of independent power.

Dad can't inject these, and dad's presence corrupts the kid's experience and dilutes the eventual sense of power. Why?

Because dad is THERE.

Personal check: Are you muttering that you can do it, even though most dads fail? What makes you specially gifted for success in this challenge?

Leading isn't coaching. Successful leaders focus first on what their business needs. Part of that is choosing and developing ("coaching") key leaders, but the searing truth is that the job requires pushing out people who can't do their jobs. Every leader I've worked with has confessed that they "waited too long" to move out a poor performer. " Perform or move out" is not the foundation for healthy coaching.

Coaching asks a different question: Who are you, and how can we develop your skills to benefit you and our company? Positive reinforcement beats fear in skills development, even though fear of failure is an essential driver.

The quandary is dad's agenda, and the exquisite balance of learning and performance is easily corrupted in the habits of business success. The company always looms, skewing the coaching dynamic.

Real practice isn't available. Mid-size firms have few leadership positions, and most aren't available to groom a future leader. Learning the ropes of the business — the details of production, shipping, cash flow, selling, and so forth — isn't the same as learning leadership.

The Other Side of Succession

Here's how it looks:

ACCELERANT: What is your kid's plan to develop him or herself?

Chapter 23
How Dads Successfully Teach Their Kids to Be CEO

"I had no idea it was this hard." David was a 40-year-old CEO of a substantial family business. He'd worked there for 20 years, in most departments. He was bright, conscientious, and driven to excel. His parents were sharp and caring, with little family drama. After three years as CEO, David still struggled, discovering that his experience in the business was insufficient to become its leader.

This experience almost derailed the career of an exceptional CEO. His subsequent success came from intense outside help coupled with his own hard work. Until then he didn't know what he didn't know, and wrongly thought the problem was his aptitude.

David encapsulates the dad's challenge: How can a son or daughter learn to be the CEO that the company needs for the future?

It would be nice to borrow a page from the few large firms who successfully grow replacement CEOs.

But those organizations provide these elements, all out of

reach of smaller firms:
- Graduated practice in a series of leadership positions.
- Multiple coaches and advisors.
- Guardrails to enable real risk without catastrophe.

SPEED BUMP: Mid-size firms must make up their own path to grow a CEO.

There are some proven ways to find that path, however. Here are three minimum steps, worthwhile regardless of whether he or she ultimately succeeds you as CEO. (Sadly, they are the same for pretty much all learning):

Step 1: Observe
- Enlarge your field of role models.
- Watch how other superb leaders do it (don't just listen to them describe it).
- Craft situations that enable watching and discussion.
- Agree out loud that watching and discussion can happen frequently. (This is the other reason for him or her to work in another organization.)

This is not the usual mentorship, which focuses more on how to succeed in one organization.

Step 2: Practice
More vital than observation, real trial situations are critical. To be effective levers of leadership growth, they require these minimums:
- Individual leadership of others: Be part of a team, become their leader because of your contributions, and do it out of your father's sight.
- Consequences that matter.
- Chances to fail and adjust.
- Multiple opportunities to lead people, one-on-one.

SPEED BUMP: The core of effective leadership is one-to-one.

Step 3: Be Coached
An outside look and individualized skill training beats self-teaching. To be most successful, a coach must have played the game and be gifted in teaching fundamentals to someone else. Sideline analysis from a nonplayer is a weak second choice, because winning details are seldom seen by an observer who has learned only by watching.

My Stanford MBA provided unsurpassed analytical and teamwork skills, but I learned to lead in proverbial trial-by-fire situations—by doing it in demanding leadership positions under the critical eye of veteran (intimidating) senior executives who had skin in the game.

When I was tasked with developing and implementing a new concept bakery in 30 Chicago locations (of a multibillion-dollar firm), I failed to get approval in my initial presentation to the corporate executive leadership team. They insisted that I identify the major risks in the project, and at least provide initial solution steps. But I didn't want to admit any weakness or problem in the plan, missing the essential need for their guidance through the inevitable problems in the path of implementation. I'll never forget the rejection—or the need to seek competent help for any major initiative. Most frustrating, this help was committed to my success, but I didn't allow myself to see it at first!

Stanford taught me well, but rejection and failure taught me a lesson I have put into practice repeatedly over the years.

SPEED BUMP: Being a successful CEO demands hands-on practice with a coach.

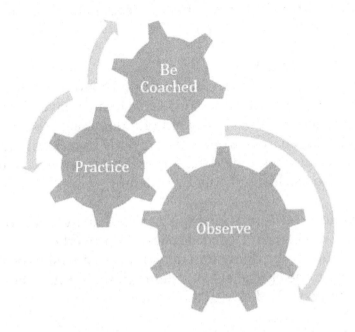

Becoming a successful CEO doesn't require magic. It does demand a willingness to jump in while being close enough to a skilled coach to prevent permanent injury to the trainee or the business.

At an architecture firm where I coached, the new Managing Principal (~CEO) was the first nonfounder in the role. After a year of work together, he delivered a profit jump that was three times the prior three-year average, with per-employee sales rising 15 percent over the prior year. He was successful because he aggressively tried things, listened, made mistakes, and learned from the pain.

SPEED BUMP: Ability passes genetically, but interest and drive may not.

ACCELERANT: What's your plan to replace yourself?

Chapter 24
Build Your Next Life

The odds of a satisfying succession plummet without the best possible legal and financial plans. Sadly, those plans alone are not enough, and ignoring the critical third aspect of the plans leads to pain and disappointment.

The third aspect is actually stepping through the door, from business insider to business outsider. Regardless of the frame of the new position, it's not like the old one. Worse, excellent financial planning provides an illusion of control, which makes this next phase potentially more shocking.

SPEED BUMP: When you exit your business, all you can do is watch.

This change from business insider to business outsider is tricky. Few leaders accept the reality that as they step out of the CEO position, regardless of their new role, the shock will be like a stun gun. Prior success is no protection, because there is no perfectly clear vision, other than to repeat their current job in another place.

Listen to 54-year-old NFL legend John Elway, who wears two Super Bowl rings as he tries to build a Super Bowl winner as GM of the Denver Broncos: "'That first colonoscopy was a marker.' [But the real jolt came five months ago, when he became a grandfather.] "That's the one where I said, 'Wow, I am starting to get up there.'" According to the article in Fortune magazine, Elway "feels far more responsibility — and far less control — than he did as a player. Come Sundays, all he can do is watch."*

Look closely, because your situation mirrors Elway's when you step through the door. Elway is driving to win as intensely as ever, but he finds himself in a strange country with rules that he's struggling to learn.

SPEED BUMP: Don't assume that past success will float you to the top next time.

Your next-phase life plan is critical. Build it with the same intensity that built your business. It will be new to you in ways that shock you:

• Your past experience may fund the courage to step out, but wealth and uncertainty can cripple your ability to go for the new excitement awaiting you.

• Unless you have successfully started or taken over at least three different businesses, the scale of change can easily overwhelm your confidence, your wealth, and your chance of success.

• Unless you'll be satisfied to golf and travel the rest of your life, this can feel like stepping into a dark elevator shaft. Change often feels like loss, because real loss always accompanies change. We easily prepare for the "loss" of the business, but don't always prepare for the other — the loss of not being the CEO.

*Fortune, February 1, 2015

One of my most successful clients worked with his father to transition leadership of their company. The transition was a success — after five years. The change for the father was as dramatic as for his son, as both found themselves as "strangers in a strange land" (to borrow the words of science-fiction writer Robert Heinlein).

SPEED BUMP: Beyond the door is destruction of your support system and your sense of accomplishment.

What is the prescription for the vibrant life that can await you for 20 years plus? Here's a start, assuming that you'll be massively unprepared for the destruction of your support system, measures, feedback, and sense of accomplishment:

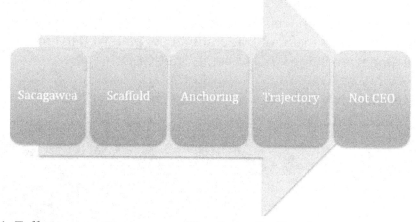

1. Follow your **Sacagawea**. Shoshone Indian Sacajawea was an essential guide and interpreter for the success of Lewis & Clark's journey as explorers. Your new life is about as unknown as the western United States that Lewis & Clark set out to discover. Get a guide.

2. Build the **scaffold** for your new routine. Replace the life framework provided by your business with a new frame-

work of goals, actions, and considered learning.

3. Develop **anchoring** practices to counter being out of control. Clarify what matters most to you now, and build in actions that help you return to grab it. Building the required habit is the stuff of years, not weeks.

4. Define your new **trajectory** now, from CEO to new life. The trajectory has three parts:
- Describe your target life 24 months after you leave your current position.
- List actions to move toward the target after you leave.
- Begin "target actions" that you can take while you're still in the business.

Most leaders plan well for transfer of assets. Some do limited planning for transfer of leadership. Few plan well to cross the line from being CEO to being "not-CEO."

ACCELERANT: How will you cross the line?

Chapter 25
Life after Succession

Every business has a succession event. Yes, even yours. For once let's move the focus past the event to life afterward. No, this is not a paean to the joys of the retirement trio: reading, travel, and golf. Instead, let's make this your second midlife crisis, with a nod to golf.

My golf pro drove me nuts insisting that I "finish the swing." Good advice, hard to do since I couldn't see myself. I thought I was following through beyond belief; instead, I stopped short. Repeatedly. I stopped short because it felt like I was finished. The advice is the same for tennis, baseball, windsurfing, track, or push-ups: Push past what you think is the end. Run through the tape. Better results are guaranteed.

Here's an example of the payoff for running through the tape: It took three weeks to figure out how to cut waste dramatically at a successful company where I worked, and three months to make the cuts stick. Analysis:
1. First part of the race: Figure out a solution.
2. Push through the tape: Help others bring it to life.
3. Result: Annualized savings boosted profit 50 percent!

SPEED BUMP: Success requires running through the tape.

The Other Side of Succession

Here's your first quiz: Which of these accurately describes succession?
1. Replace the leadership.
2. Replace the ownership.
3. Shut down.

Answer: Any of the above.

Here's a stunner: No matter which of these occurs, there is a post-succession phase (PSP). Even better, you can influence that PSP dramatically, if you start now.

SPEED BUMP: A good finish seldom overcomes a bad start.

Just as sprints are often decided by the start, your PSP can be dramatically better if you start wisely.

Here's an assessment to get you started: Rank the following list in importance to your post-succession business. Note which is #2 in importance. (Yes, all are vital, but some are more vital than others.)

• Capital
• People
• Leadership
• Execution
• Niche (who buys from you and why)

Okay, this is a trick question. The #2 factor for PSP is always Leadership, because just as the perfect car is useless without a driver, an organization depends on leadership to survive. Always. (And #1 is whatever you choose).

SPEED BUMP: The best successions start with the best leaders after succession.

124

Instead of just letting the next person pick the leader (and the leadership team), why don't you do it? You understand the business better than anyone. You are at least as good as the next person at picking people. If you pick the leadership team far enough ahead of the succession event, you can groom them to dramatically improve their odds of success. You don't even need to know where the business will go ten years after your succession. If you build the right leaders, they'll figure that out for you, with a little advice from you. Wouldn't you rather be an investor/advisor than an owner-manager?

If not, we need to talk.

So where's the crisis (as in second midlife crisis)? It's in handing over real decisions to anyone else. As long as you're the CEO, no matter how you empower your key folks, they look to you for conscious and unconscious guidance. That guidance frequently happens without you knowing it. Each of your leaders knows what you'll accept and what won't fly, whether they talk with you about it or not. While you're CEO, that's hyper efficient, usually effective, and provides you with enormous daily comfort.

Since you're now looking past the tape to boost your PSP, which of these styles of CEO change will you endorse?

1. Just Leave. It feels like freedom to you, but leaving succession to the folks you left behind creates enormous risk to your future income and the success of the business.
2. Gradual Grooming. This takes thought and patience, as the power and initiative dance evolves, but when done well it's a powerhouse driver for success.
3. Sell & Go. (An outsider is brought in to run the business). Regardless of how you imagine it, the effect on the business,

including employees and customers, is dangerously unpredictable. Why? Because an outsider who isn't groomed into the business brings her own values and goals, and they may be dangerously different from yours.

How do you want to build your PSP?

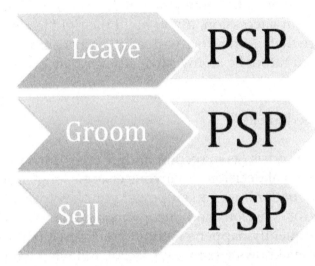

ACCELERANT: Will you create your own Post-Succession with the care and skill that you brought to the business?

Chapter 26
The Succession Promise

Succession offers the excitement of early company growth with the comfort of years of winning. (If that weren't true, there would be no succession discussion.) It's another step into unknown territory, a familiar experience. As before, preparing a little and adjusting a lot promises the best chance of dramatic success.

SPEED BUMP: Your early hand in succession boosts the odds of later success.

Succession will happen with or without you. If you're in it ahead of time, you win the fun and satisfaction of crossing this finish line with an energy boost into your future. You'll likely have more assets to put into play as well.

Here are two succession stories to send you on your way. One firm planned ahead, and the other recovered after the succession.

Planning Ahead
The owners of a trash hauling company invested in boosting their firm's profitability, a tough task in a highly regulated industry. We looked inside their operations, finding ways for their drivers to safely leave work when their routes were

finished. The safety framework measured and rewarded reductions in the three major risks of the business: personal accidents, missed customer pickups, and vehicle accidents. Letting drivers go home when they were done revealed true route times, enabling accurate re-routing that boosted net worth 20 percent.

This work anticipated that the owners' son would take over the business. When he elected a different career, the business sold for a premium that exceeded the owners' dreams. Today, they live on a small farm, travel around the region to watch their son race their racing cars, and enjoy their grandchildren and friends.

Recovery after Succession
The other company planned for succession but undertrained their son in the skills to continue the company's growth. When we met, he had been CEO for three years. Company results were so weak that he said, "I had no idea that this job is so hard!" Strikingly, his parents, founders of a successful firm, had invested over 20 years in carefully exposing him to all aspects of the business. He had that foundational knowledge of how things worked, but he had limited skill in the complex leadership tasks of a CEO. Watching his parents and talking about it wasn't enough.

Happily, we worked together to build his leadership skills and self-confidence, and today the firm is so profitable that its 14-month backlog is driving an expansion plan that will double or triple the size of the business in coming years. The doubt and pain of this recovery make a strong case for the planning we've described in this book.

SPEED BUMP: In succession, good planning can deliver remarkable results.

ACCELERANT: Will you take your first succession step this week?

Part 6 Post-Succession Success

Chapter 27
The Art of Departure

Departing for a CEO, especially a veteran, can look a lot like the actions of the rufous-sided towhee – a seven-inch bird that hops, scratches, climbs trees, and pokes around for its food. The bird is seldom still, and its path is unpredictable. Similarly, a departing CEO has so much to manage that it can look uncoordinated to the outsider.

Here's a menu of the departing CEO's challenges:

1. Keep the business performing: Even though everyone (employees, customers, and suppliers) eventually knows that the CEO is leaving.

2. Keep key leaders inspired, with their shoulders to the wheel: They can't help looking around to see what's going to change, who the new leader will be, what the new rules will look like, and so forth, yet they have to get on with the work.

3. Keep suppliers pushing for good service: Suppliers are hypersensitive to problem customers, who may be slow to pay, change specifications unreasonably, cut prices, demand new services, and so forth. There are many reasons to slow down, step back, and size up what the new relationship might mean, even before there's a new leader.

4. Keep customers happy: When the leadership door opens a crack, legacy customer problems seem to burst forth vigorously, seeking either reassurance or better terms and service. Worse, prospects may delay committing to new orders until they can see the shape of the new leadership.

5. Keep employees committed and focused: Unlike top leaders, they value security and consistency above almost anything else, and a new leader threatens both.

6. Build a working relationship with the new CEO: It's a myth that the departing CEO disappears into the ether, like a fog.

SPEED BUMP: Where will you get the support that this vast change demands?

What's the success formula? Shift your picture from driving (or pulling) people to succeed, to supporting and helping them in their daily work. Their feelings want reassurance that things will be okay (and that they will be too). Although you can't guarantee that (and never have been able to), you can still provide critical support as they carry on.

Here are three factors in the success formula:

1. Communicate. Immediately after announcing your departure, volunteer your answers to these questions:
- Why are you leaving?
- Will the business work without you?
- Will you be available for advice?

2. Listen. Shift most of your time to face-to-face listening.

Move to the agenda of the other person by asking them questions. Stop, sit down, and look at them. Drink deeply of who they are, just as you would if they were your top sales prospect. Answer as little as possible, except where you are certain of your answers. It's okay that they know that you don't know either. (Who can predict the future?)

In one of the companies where I worked, the founder was a crusty guy who shot straight, sometimes with collateral damage. He was revered by folks in the firm. After his retirement he would show up unannounced, and word of him flew through the people like a whirlwind. The lift in their step and firmer set of their chins was visible, regardless of their position or even their relationship to him. He represented a reliable guy in the fight with them, bringing powerful insights and encouragement to do better. Even though he had left the company, he never left their hearts, and that seemed to be as they wanted it to be.

3. Own your limits. It's awkward to move suddenly from driver to passenger, even though we see it daily. That transition can have these steps:

-Back-Seat Driver: Nervously calling out instructions to a driver who may ignore them.

-Back-Seat Mutterer: Same instructions mumbled under his breath. An uncomfortable passenger for everyone in the car.

-Delighted Passenger: Happy to be along for the ride, curious about the trip, offering comfortable support and gratitude for the driver.

SPEED BUMP: Which kind of passenger will you be?

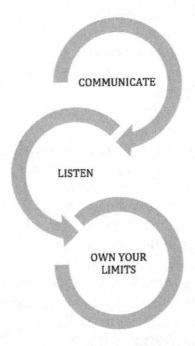

Here's the payday: Look after the new CEO like she was your own daughter. That means consciously letting her do things you disagree with, sometimes violently. That means checking in and listening, for the sole purpose of supporting her. Remember that when you were CEO, there were precious few folks who could listen with enough knowledge and patience to be safely helpful. You can do that, if you will.

ACCELERANT: When do you start listening with support and patience?

The departing CEO has a powerful stake in the success of the incoming CEO and the company's future. So read on.

Jim Grew

Chapter 28
Accelerate Success after Succession

Since there is life after succession, here are some beginning ideas for your successors. When the time draws near, you might consider sharing this postlude with them.

Stepping up or in to a new CEO role is exhilarating until the first meeting with the board, CFO, or leadership team. It may not be Halloween, but the surprises will be surprising. The opportunities will be dwarfed by the immediate problems that were always there, but somehow stayed under control.

SPEED BUMP: Like lottery winners, long-lost issues show up with their hands out.

Let's read some of the fine print.

Double Burden — The thousands of post-succession leaders carry a double burden:

1. Leading others: Leadership exacts a heavy price for those who fail to balance vision and execution — not by themselves, but by their people. The delicate art of moving and re-balancing offers great rewards, and threatens crushing penalties for those who get it wrong. The re-balancing part is the back side of vision: it is progress with the people and resources available in the moment.

SPEED BUMP: Success is a little vision and a lot of balanced effort.

2. Completing the succession: Just because there's a new leader with skill, energy, and vision, there's no guarantee the company will survive, let alone flourish. Changing leaders at the top is like major surgery (not a hip replacement, but heart surgery): the outcome is usually worth it, but things will never be the same and recovery includes large dollops of pain. When the new CEO has been promoted from within, it improves the odds a bit but doesn't address the invisible tendons and nerve endings of the company.

SPEED BUMP: Resilience may outrank effectiveness in the first year.

Challenges — Depending on where the new leader comes from, particular challenges arise:

•**From within the company:** The promotion is like cresting a mountain in the jungle. The outlook is bracing, and successful return is an overpowering challenge. As one of my clients said, "I had no idea how hard this is." The problem is that most new CEOs continue to do what made them successful, ignoring the discomfort of changing what they do and how they do it. Without adjusting to the re-quirements of their new job, they'll fail in confusion, after working harder than they've worked in their life.

• **From outside the company:** Even if the newbie masters the culture, he'll race failure in building these requirements for success:

Replacing Leaders: Restructuring for the future is common, and changing a few key leaders is frequent. Both are especially difficult for outsiders to do well. The deep, detailed information needed to reduce the chance of error in these choices is elusive, and personal agendas of other leaders necessarily influence the information and the decisions. That influence is not always best for the business.

Communication: The communication essential for success as a top leader is up from below, not down from the top. Fiercely filtered, that data is often late, off the mark, or colored with personal fears. Building a reliable network of folks who provide information takes longer than initial key decisions allow, increasing the risk of a mistake.

Sources of information: MBAs and accountants to the contrary, numbers usually don't mean what they say. Their data can be essential, but its inputs and compromises for time or clarity make obscurity likely. Veterans of the organization adjust analysis and action through the sieve of experience. Outsiders' sieves have holes that are too large, in the early months.

One of my many humbling experiences was leading a truck tank manufacturing firm. We installed the tank and equipment on truck bodies to make gasoline, diesel, and propane trucks. It took two years and a forensic accounting investigation to disclose why we weren't making much money. I should have picked it up in three months, but missed it. The founder, who had sold his company to the investors I worked for, made all his money buying and selling trucks (he owned three truck dealerships). There was no margin in installing commodity tanks and pumping systems! The fact that he fooled three practiced investors was little consolation.

ACCELERANT: New CEOs: Will you listen a lot and do a little for a long time?

Chapter 29
Rules for the Next CEO

Much is made of the succession puzzle for owners, leaving the prospective successor CEO wondering exactly how to fit in when the founder is present. A clear understanding of the puzzle pieces is what the new CEO needs to function effectively and put the big picture together.

Solving the succession puzzle for owners includes laying groundwork for future success. That groundwork builds upon anticipating the requirements for the next CEO's success, and erecting a bridge to help meet those requirements.

Here are three critical pieces for the new CEO to handle expertly:

Piece 1: The Aura of "Dad"
The founder or long-time CEO is in the minds of every employee, regardless of their individual position or history. What's the same for all is the refrain, "What would he do?" (WWHD). The intensity varies with the situation and the person, but it's built into the daily choices that every employee makes to do their job. It's double-blind, crafted from individual experience and perspective, tough to see and manage.

The Other Side of Succession

A few tips to use the aura constructively:

• Assume that it's always present. The habit of WWHD lives quietly in most people.

• Use it to power success. Most successful businesses do many things right. It's the art of leadership to harness the culture's power in order to methodically upgrade performance in the nuts and bolts of daily operation.

• Borrow it to see beneath the surface. When you find a situation that doesn't make sense to you, ask the two key probes:
    - Why is that?
    - What's the evidence for that?

SPEED BUMP: A new CEO doesn't erase "Dad" — it gives him new life in the minds of your people.

Piece 2: Shifting Power with the Prior CEO
The power dance for the new CEO will be different from any that she's experienced before. Both the old and the new CEO want the new one to be successful quickly. Both folks are driven by their different habits, experiences, and expectations as they craft this relationship, however. Those differences yield different pictures of how things should work between them.

Insights for quick success:

• Treat the former CEO as a fellow searcher, not as an authority or a relic. Each of you is building a relationship that's so new that it's not in any book or any past experience.
• Practice patient listening and questioning to understand; genuine understanding will be more valuable than negotiating a quick path forward.

• Data will unlock both your doors to the future. It's your job to collect it.

• Don't wait for the former CEO to act. Go see for yourself, and then check your data and conclusions out with him. You've got an expert right beside you; use him.

• This relationship will change at an unexpected pace, much like working with your infant as she lives from three months to three years old. The change is constant; the future unexpected.

SPEED BUMP: Let yourself learn at the same fierce rate as when you started to work.

When I ran a business for the founder, it took us too long to clarify who was working on the overlap questions. His focus was sales and finance, but we waited too long to poke the product development team to ramp up their output. Each of us thought the other was taking it on, but progress didn't happen until he and I talked about it, crafted an approach to a sensitive product development leader, and worked to help him meet his deadlines. Our lack of proactive communication on the issue unnecessarily hurt sales and profit.

Piece 3: Timely Action That the Business Requires
While you are trying to figure out the pieces and the complexity of your relationship with the Aura and the former CEO, the business piece will tug constantly at your sleeve. You will see problems that aren't what they appear; you'll feel responsible for situations beyond your control; and your inbox will flood at lightning speed. You'll be torn between respecting the Aura (WWHD) and stepping in to take action. Often when that happens it's time to pause and talk together, to clarify the path to action.

145

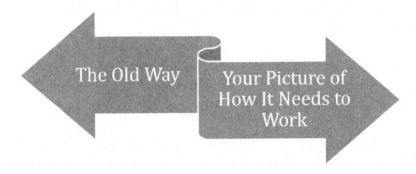

The windows forward:

• Do less than you think you need to do. Your prime job is to see that you have the right people doing the right things. Your next job is to master the outside world that your business lives in. Use your advisor (former CEO) for a contrasting point of view, not an answer.

• Focus on what your key people are doing, and how you can help them up their game. Information for you is like water to a fish — it's survival.

• Ward off your drive to do this job exactly like you did the last one. Many of your shortcuts and essential skills are now out of date.

ACCELERANT: What does your piece of this puzzle look like?

Chapter 30
Exquisite Pacing

Goal alignment is a useful but tired leadership cliché, refer-
ring to employees and leaders aiming consistently at similar
goals. But when there's a new CEO, pacing frequently suf-
fers, as the new leader wants to go faster or slower than her
familiar predecessor. Mastering pacing — and making adjustments to it — is a vital success skill that's often overlooked by
new leaders anxious to make their mark.

For a fresh look, what if we focus on gait alignment instead
of pacing? Gait? That's how people (and animals) move over
the ground. For our purpose, it's how your people move
forward (or not).

The concept has been memorialized in harness racing, a
carefully choreographed type of horse racing with a small
buggy for the jockey. Of the two types of gait in harness racing, pacers are faster than trotters, because they can extend
their legs farther. Yes, their stride is bigger. Their capacity
for speed is designed in, if you will.

SPEED BUMP: Your job as leader is to pace your team for
top performance.

How can you "design in" faster progress among your team?

149

The Other Side of Succession

Strangely, it's not by going faster. It's by moving more slowly than your people. That essential skill is one of the three foundations for successfully accelerating the pace of your team.

Think of a NASCAR pace car (or "safety car"):

• It drives slower than its top speed, unlike the race cars on the track.
• No car may pass it.
• Its job is to contain the speed of the race cars for two reasons: 1) to enable a safe and fair start and 2) to allow time for the track to be cleared of dangerous debris.

The various teams in businesses must all move at about the same pace, otherwise they will make mistakes, generate waste, and do a lousy job with customers. For example, the design team serves as a pace car: Too fast produces mistakes, delays, and re-work. Too slow misses customer orders. And its output is meaningless until it's turned into products and sold.

Most top leaders were promoted partly because of their work as individuals, including fast results, close attention to priorities, and devotion to the details that mattered. Most leaders find that their problem-solving pace slows when they become CEO, as the range of issues they face broadens. They still work quickly, but their speed is in setting priorities and recruiting teams and individuals to dispatch problems or seize opportunities. Their own problem-solving pace must match or slightly exceed their organization's slowest, or they'll unbalance their teams like a bobsled team leaning in different directions.

SPEED BUMP: Go slower than you did when you worked alone.

Sustainable speed builds on a foundation like the one below. You may need to help teams see this for each problem:

Alignment: What will success look like? Ask out loud, for answers in writing. Discuss and modify until there's enthusiastic agreement (including you).

Details: What details are critical to success? Most details allow greater wiggle room than is acknowledged out loud. Instead, guide the team to identify the few critical details, and find a way to track them in front of everyone.

London's Heathrow Airport is one of the world's most crowded. When spacing between landing planes was set by time instead of distance, capacity rose as much as 18 percent! Here's what they did: Spacing by time enabled adjustment for headwinds, which otherwise slowed traffic as much as 19 percent. The space between planes remained the same, measured by distance, but their speed dropped in the face of the headwinds that notoriously delay Heathrow airplanes. Instead, measuring by time enabled moving the planes closer in headwinds, restoring the lost time. Surprisingly, headwinds clear out wake vortices faster than normal, enabling closer landing. Wake vortices, the violently swirling winds generated by flying airliners, were thought to be so dangerous as to prevent landing planes closer together. Detailed study showed differently. Vive la details!

Adjustment: Quick, finely tuned adjustments will boost your team's speed. Race cars and planes use a feedback loop for guidance. Here's how your team can apply its principles immediately:

The Other Side of Succession

1. Evidence: What do we know right now?
2. Relevance: How does it impact our performance?
3. Consequence: What happens if we respond to it — or not?
4. Action: What do we do now?

Here's how it can spotlight a powerful next action:

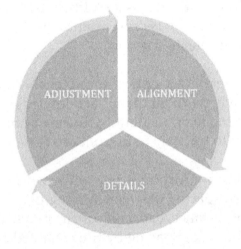

SPEED BUMP: It's not how fast your people can work individually; it's their top sustainable speed together.

ACCELERANT: What's your team's fastest sustainable speed?

Now What Will You Do?

This book is written for leaders like John, who happens to be one of my favorite clients. John is a second-generation successful leader of a vital business founded by his dad. Recently past his 52nd birthday, John says that he wants three things:

1. He doesn't want to sell, at least not anytime soon.
2. He doesn't want to be like his dad, who stayed too long as leader, damaging his life, his health, and the business in his later years.
3. He wants to stay involved in the business at a gradually reduced level of intensity.

John loves working in the business, and he has a gleam in his eye as he imagines the next growth spurt that's just around the corner (really). Wouldn't you like to feel that way? Well then why don't you do what John is doing?

He's building an action plan to make the next 15 years of his life what he wants it to be. John has discovered that the stakes are high, since it involves his time, his pleasure, his money, his family, and his future, in areas that are new to him. High stakes usually call for expert help, since the questions can be new and the life consequences dramatic.

John is reviewing his stable of advisors, checking for their current expertise in the basic issues in this change. If they've little experience in rapid growth and change in ownership and fundamental leadership, he will look for experts who have done these things for others like him.

SPEED BUMP: Hubris and naiveté can be lethal here.

Here is his action checklist, designed to move him from owner-manager to investor. It's a great checklist for you too:

Review current advisors

Seek new advisors

Frame action plan

Here are the details:

• **Review current advisors.** Actively confirm that key advisors have current experience in business ownership change. That includes issues relating to the business, key executives, family, personal assets, tax planning, and legal structuring. If any of these advisors doesn't have current experience in guiding these changes for similar business owners, look for advisors who have that experience.

• **Seek additional advisors.** This business situation is new, since it combines a push for growth with plans for major changes in key leadership. These changes point to the future, not the past, and may include expert help in areas such as these:

- Business strategy and implementation
- Revising leadership structure, leadership roles, and management disciplines.
- Capital structure
- Tax strategy
- Financial Reporting for the future

- **Frame an initial action plan with each advisor.**
    - Combine a detailed picture of your desired future five to seven years out with an action list for the next 24 months. The action plan should consider issues such as these (and this list is not complete):

SPEED BUMP: The top failure risk is underestimating how unfamiliar all this is.

1. **Legal Plan**, including issues such as:
    a. Personal estate plans
    b. Family trusts
    c. Business structure and clear ownership
    d. Framework for planned changes in ownership
    e. Compensation for key executives and family

2. Personal Financial Plan, including issues such as:
  a. Managing current assets for self and family
  b. Planning for adjustments in asset ownership
  c. Income planning for changes related to changes in work compensation
  d. Investment planning for future capital income
  e. Lifestyle planning

3. Tax Plan, including issues such as:
  a. Optimizing tax reporting within the business
  b. Shifting from minimizing business tax to other goals
  c. Updating individual plans and structures to minimize future taxes
  d. Considering revised ownership structures to minimize taxes

4. Business Financial Reporting, including issues such as:
  a. Shifting to Compiled financial statements next fiscal year
  b. Shifting to Reviewed financial statements the following fiscal year
  c. Shifting to Audited GAAP financial statements the following three years
  d. Instantiating changes suggested to make these statements reliable to outsiders, whether they are purchasers or sources of capital for growth or risk reduction. ("taking some chips off the table," in common parlance)

SPEED BUMP: Growth at this stage is counterintuitive, and takes extra discipline.

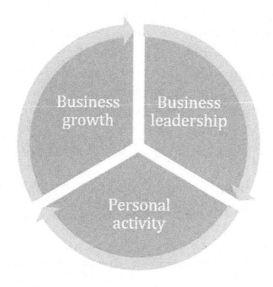

5. Business Growth plan, including issues such as:
   a. Strategic growth overview
   b. Specific growth sources, with required investment and projected outcomes
   c. Twin levels of growth strategy, including likely and "stretch" goals
   d. Capital plan
   e. Cash flow plan

6. Business Leadership Transition Plan, including issues such as:
   a. Desired leadership structure in five years
   b. People development plan for internal and external candidates
   c. Information transfer plan from senior leaders to potential successors
   d. Incentives for current leaders to drive needed changes

7. Personal Activity Plan: Specific changes in what you do each day, and what you are responsible for. Those changes create your path from today to your future state in five to seven years. It should include answers to these questions:

    a. **Creation:** What new work would you like to do, and how can you get there?

    b. **Elimination:** When can you eliminate or delegate work you don't like?

    c. **Preserving:** What should you keep, and for how long?

    d. **Accepting:** What do you know you need to give up, but struggle to do so?

ACCELERANT: What is your path to your future?

Glossary of Financial Terms

These practical definitions are to help you understand basic concepts of business accounting and finance in this book. They are for general guidance, and do not replace the detailed analysis of a competent CPA.

assets: All things of value owned or controlled and paid for by the business. Examples include:
• Short-term assets such as cash and working capital assets (accounts receivable, inventory)
• Long-term capital property and equipment
• Leases — A capital lease is a "right of use" asset because value is conferred through usage, not ownership.
Most assets are resources the firm bought or created. They are recorded in a business's books at cost less usage, or lower of cost or market. "Usage" may include items such as depreciation or devaluation of bad inventory or receivables.

cash flow: Not the same as profit, cash flow is a measure of cash generated minus cash used for a time period.

EBITDA: This acronym is a customary measure of a business's core performance. It estimates cash flows generated by a business in a year — after paying all expenses and collecting all customer bills, after adding back non-cash expenses (depreciation and amortization). It is customarily used in privately held businesses. Sometimes capital expense and taxes are also deducted to clarify performance.

Its elements are explained below:

E: Earnings — Revenues (top line) minus all expenses — all costs incurred — to earn those revenues and to keep the business going, regardless of whether these sales are collected or expenses paid.

B: Before costs of interest, taxes, depreciation, and amortization.

I: Interest — Interest expense, the interest accrued for rent of money on any form of financing, such as long-term and short-term debt.

T: Taxes — Income taxes on the operating profit, paid or not.

D: Depreciation — This is an estimate of the cost of using a long-term asset over its useful life, but not because that asset is losing value on the market. It is also used to calculate a tax deduction. It has nothing to do with the market value of the asset but literally is a fraction of what you paid for that equipment or building for a year so that you can estimate profit in one year, even if the equipment or building lasts longer. Government authorities determine the depreciation rates for income taxes.

A: Amortization — This is like depreciation for intangible assets that are "purchased" (i.e., bought from outside, not created internally). Examples of intangibles that could appear in a business's books and be amortized include the cost of acquiring a franchise or license, the cost of registering a trademark, or the cost of purchasing such assets from another company. The time period for write-off depends on the type of asset, but usually is the shortest period possible, or useful life. It is best to have advice from your accountant about the amortization rate, which is defined also by law for tax purposes

equity: Total assets minus total liabilities, less how much creditors own of these assets. Equity is your net worth, part of which the owners contributed to the company and part of which the company earned. To maximize value you want to maximize the part earned and retained in the company. For example, your equity in your home is what you paid for it, minus what you owe on your mortgage. It has nothing to do with market value.

expenses: The cost of doing business, including the cost of goods sold, labor used in operations, and all other costs incurred to operate—sales and marketing, R & D, and all administrative expense, whether these costs are paid or not.

GAAS: The common set of accounting principles, standards, and procedures that companies use to compile their financial statements. GAAS (Generally Accepted Accounting Standards) are a combination of authoritative standards (set by policy boards) and the commonly accepted ways of recording and reporting accounting information (Investopedia. com). GAAS rules are commonly applied by public companies for all financial reporting, but private firms often apply them only as part of year-end tax preparation.

levels of financial statements: CPA firms can provide three types of assistance or assurance in preparing financial statements: compilation, review, and audit. Here is an informal explanation of the main differences.

1. Compiled financial statements — The most basic level, often used in small and mid-sized firms. They are prepared without assurance from a qualified outside professional (CPA) that the information fairly represents the condition of the firm. No audits or review checks are performed, other than those done by the staff preparing the statements. Management is responsible for the validity of these statements. These statements are usually adequate for day-to-day operations in smaller firms, though they may be adjusted to comply with tax reporting requirements at year end.

2. Reviewed financial statements — Reviewed statements add CPA analysis and inquiries to management's financial data to provide limited assurance that there are no material modifications needed for the statements to fairly represent the condition of the firm. These inquiries do not include assessing the financial risks such as those listed below under audited statements. Some banks will require reviewed statements to initiate loans, or to clarify potential problem situations.

3. Audited statements — Audited financial statements add active review by a CPA to reviewed statements. That review is based on evidence from inquiry, physical inspection, observation, third-party confirmation, examination, analytical procedures, and other methods. It enables the auditor to provide a professional opinion as to whether the statements present fairly, in all material aspects, the condition of the firm, applying the standards generally accepted in the United States (GAAS). Audited statements add testing and validation with external evidence to the internal tests required for reviewed statements.

The value of "assurance" may include the benefits listed below:
- Safeguarding assets
- Providing information to enable effective management
- Reliable data for insiders and outsiders who have interests in the firm, including owners, their families, investors, partners, lenders, bankers, and potential buyers
- Lower cost of capital
- Improved access to capital
- Potentially enhanced value at time of sale

The larger the company, the more external users look to the data, and the more important reliability becomes.

Here's what matters: Any knowledgeable investor, whether a buyer or lender, will evaluate his investment risk partly on the reliability of the financial information available to him. Moving from compiled to reviewed to audited statements improves the likelihood that the statements fairly report the condition of the firm. This may reduce the perceived risk of investment and enable more favorable terms from an investor, or enable the sale itself. Profitability, cost of capital, and price & terms of sale often improve with assurance that financial reports accurately portray the business.

liabilities: Liabilities are monies owed to suppliers, bankers, and any other creditors, including accounts payable and short-term and long-term debt, such as loans, lines of credit, and accumulated interest. They are measured at a point in time.

M & A: Mergers and acquisitions. A summary label for the activity of buying or selling a business, as well as the professional focus of specialists in these transactions.

multiple: How much someone else is willing to pay as function of the estimated cash flows they think they would realize from running your business. EBITDA is a common method of estimating cash flow for this purpose. So if the multiplier is 4, we are saying the buyer expects to collect 4 times EBITDA at current value.

operating profit: Often calculated as EBIT (EBITDA without deducting taxes, interest, depreciation, and amortization).

revenue: The top line, what you make from selling your product or services, whether the revenues are collected or not.

valuation: What your business is worth, if you were to sell on the open market. Frequently calculated as a multiple of annual EBITA, though sometimes calculated on other variables such as revenue or number of customers. For example:
- EBITDA: $1,200,000
- Multiple: 4
- Valuation: $4,800,0000

About the Author

Jim Grew is known as the Business Transition Defogger and Accelerator. He has worked in 23 companies at the C-level and is considered an expert in strategy and executive leadership. He helps leaders discover the hidden opportunities within their businesses and exploit them for dramatic results.

Jim holds an MBA degree from Stanford University and ran nine thriving businesses before he started consulting.

He regularly shares his insights in his Executive Letter: Do Business Faster™. Jim gets results for his clients:

• One company sold for 4 times more than it would have before---a difference of several million dollars.

• The net worth of another increased 20% in two years (and the owner got to take his first vacation in 11 years).

• One CEO he worked with said, "You helped us get out of the weeds and our operating profits are up a million dollars over last year."

Contact Jim
www.Grewco.com   Jim@grewco.com   503 544-8857

CPSIA information can be obtained
at www.ICGtesting.com
Printed in the USA
FSOW04n0628060617
34786FS